SANCTUARY

SANCTUARY

GARDENING FOR THE SOUL

photography by DENCY KANE

text by LAURI BRUNTON *and* ERIN FOURNIER

FRIEDMAN/FAIRFAX
PUBLISHERS

A FRIEDMAN/FAIRFAX BOOK

©1999 by Michael Friedman Publishing Group, Inc.

Library of Congress
Cataloging-in-Publication Data
available upon request

Kane, Dency.
    Sanctuary : gardening for the soul / photography by Dency Kane;
text by Lauri Brunton and Erin Fournier.
        p. cm.
    Includes bibliographical references.
    ISBN 1-56799-791-0
    1. Sanctuary gardens. I. Brunton, Lauri. II. Fournier, Erin.
III. Title.
    SB454.3.S25K36 1999
    712'.6—dc21
                                        99-26666
                                        CIP

Photography © Dency Kane
Editor: Susan Lauzau
Art Director: Jeff Batzli
Designer: Lori Thorn
Photography Editor: Wendy Missan
Production Manager: Camille Lee

Color separations by Colourscan Overseas Co Pte Ltd.
Printed in Singapore by KHL Printing Co. Pte. Ltd.

10 9 8 7 6 5 4 3 2 1

For bulk purchases and special sales, please contact:
Friedman/Fairfax Publishers
Attention: Sales Department
15 West 26th Street
New York, New York 10010
212/685-6610   fax 212/685-1307

Visit our website:
www.metrobooks.com

DEDICATION AND
ACKNOWLEDGMENTS

*We lovingly and respectfully dedicate this book to our mentor and friend Jean Byrne, whose
vivacious strength, generous spirit, unique vision, and literary talent are forever embedded in
our hearts. You are the definitive wild woman! Thank you.*

*Lauri wishes to acknowledge her family and especially her mother, Melissa Mayernik, for
their love and support.*

*Erin wishes to acknowledge her mother, Bonnie Baker, for all the evenings spent reading
aloud, and for letting her read under the covers, and Erma and Don Baker, who are her sanctuary.*

—LAURI BRUNTON AND ERIN FOURNIER

Thanks to editor Susan Lauzau and senior photo editor Wendy Missan for supporting and shaping the idea of **Sanctuary** *and to Michael Friedman for showcasing my photographs in such a beautifully printed book. Special thanks to: all the private garden owners and designers for their extra effort and for allowing me to photograph at the break of day when only the birds were awake; Longwood Gardens in Pennsylvania and The New York Botanical Garden, which stand out in their beauty and sense of quiet refuge; and those who made it possible to photograph at Pinewood House in Florida, Keukenhof Gardens in Holland, Tyler Arboretum in Pennsylvania, Memphis Botanical Garden, and Winterthur Gardens in Delaware.*

My consuming interest in labyrinths came from casual conversations with my friend Cathy Wilkinson Barash. Many thanks to her and Nancy Cook for pointing me in the right direction. My labyrinth search led to Sister Jo-Ann Iannotti at Wisdom House Retreat and Conference Center in Connecticut, Alex Champion in California, Pamela Mayer in Vermont, Patti Keeler on Cape Cod, and others too numerous to mention. Those who walk a labyrinth will understand the debt we owe them.

And to my partner Ginny Parker, who has taken this journey with me from beginning to end, and new puppy Max, who can't wait to explore the world.

—DENCY KANE

CONTENTS

INTRODUCTION

We all search for safety, for places to console, inspire, and renew us in times of worry or unease. These places are our sanctuaries. Once contained in holy centers—churches, temples, mosques, groves of trees, or other sacred spaces—sanctuaries were places of worship, where people communed with nature or their god in the hope of gaining surcease from their troubles. Today, we recognize the need to create our own private sanctuary spaces, which we can visit daily and adapt to our own desires, but the essential qualities that characterize a sanctuary—comfort, protection, and hope—remain the same.

In the garden, we find a space where we can feel both removed from our daily cares and connected to nature's grace. Trees with

mighty trunks and sinewy limbs spread protective arms around us; luxuriantly painted petals emit perfumes like incense; the yielding mounds of earth speak of nourishment and solace. But while nature unquestionably offers sanctuary, each of us has a unique sense of need, a set of personal preferences developed over time. We cannot name a single type of garden as the ideal sanctuary.

If we were to ask ten different people what natural setting or garden elements touch them most, we would find that there is no ultimate model. A sanctuary garden may take many forms, the mood of each space determined by the needs of its maker. There

Tucked into a lush oasis, simple garden chairs become places to observe and worship the cathedral of green.

are, however, repeating themes that we find surfacing again and again as we analyze various sanctuary gardens: color, pattern and texture, water, light and shadow, sound, scent, and structure and form. These elements occur, to greater or lesser degrees, in all well-designed gardens, and these ideas are revisited through each chapter in the book. But while these features may be present in many types of garden, it is the special and intentional arrangement of elements that creates a sanctuary space.

Some people find sanctuary in a garden setting where calming green tones and gently flowing water invite serenity. For others, a passionate garden breathes energy into their spirits with heady fragrances and striking colors. Still others find comfort in the joyful celebration of nature's changing forms and intricate cycles. Mysterious gardens, with their hints at riddles yet to be solved, awaken some visitors to the limitless possibilities of life and the potential that lies ahead. Others prefer the ambiance of a contemplative gar-

den, choosing to center on objects that draw them inward. Each of these garden themes, and indeed probably countless others, offer viable sanctuary spaces, where we can feel revived and encouraged, inspired and renewed.

In planning your own sanctuary garden, ask yourself what it is you expect from the space. What is your ideal sanctuary? Where do you feel most protected? How did the places of your childhood console or inspire you? What pleasing scents, colors,

OPPOSITE: *The fruit of a butterfly weed (Asclepias tuberosa) splits, revealing seeds attached to downy white hairs. These fluffs will drift in breezes that carry seeds to fertile soil, beginning the cycle of life all over again.* RIGHT: *Autumn's brilliant crimsons and reds remind us that gardens have a language all their own: radiant fruit and foliage are nature's elegant words and gestures.*

In the garden, we find a space where we
can feel both removed from our daily cares
and connected to nature's grace.

and shapes can you recall? Remember that a garden lends itself to endless creativity, its design limited only by your imagination. Even if your favorite childhood sanctuary was your father's study, you will be able to find ways to integrate some of the colors, scents, and ornaments of that cherished place into your garden. As you ponder your treasured memories, don't confine yourself to traditional sanctuary ideals: suspend judgment and let your thoughts run without bounds.

But it is not only the garden that is refreshing to the spirit, it is also the act of gardening. By planting and tending flowers, foliage, and vegetables, our long link with the earth, which has sustained and nourished us since the beginning of human history, is

RIGHT: *The beloved shape and glowing color of cottage tulip 'Orange Bouquet' warm us with their comforting familiarity.*
OPPOSITE: *The genius of nature may lie in its ability to continually surprise us with its beautiful spring.*

By planting and tending flowers, foliage, and vegetables,

our long link with the earth, which has sustained and

nourished us since the beginning of human history, is reestablished.

You'll see reflected in the garden,

with its daily small miracles and multitude of

interdependent lives, its unfolding growth and its inevitable tragedies,

the patterns of your own existence.

reestablished. We come to appreciate more deeply nature's sublime artistry, the careful way she lays her map. In working the earth we come upon stones chiseled by rain, snow, and wind and origami-like leaves cut by nature's daring scissors, everyday miracles we might otherwise be too busy to notice.

In the pages of this book you will find scores of images and ideas that will help you bring meaning and a sense of sanctuary to your garden. But more than that, you will find a new way of looking at the garden; you'll discover the beauties of form and pattern in the curving surface of a veiny leaf

and the splendor of light and color in the stained-glass translucence of an orange poppy petal. You'll see reflected in the garden, with its daily small miracles and multitude of interdependent lives, its unfolding growth and its inevitable tragedies, the patterns of your own existence.

Each chapter describes a garden sanctuary that embodies a particular character: peace, change, passion, mystery, and contemplation. You may wish to borrow just one or two ideas to add to your garden, or you may be inspired to create a full-scale retreat. Realize as you read that certain of

the concepts may be applicable to more than one space—gardens devoted to peace, for instance, bear similarities to those designed for contemplation, and these two themes are closely related. Take the concepts or elements that appeal to you and use them freely in your garden. Open to the photographs and passages that speak most to you. Find the threads that will help you identify and weave together the special strands of your own sanctuary garden.

Garden paths are rarely about the destination—rather, it is the walk itself that is the reward.

CHAPTER ONE

PEACE

Days begin with the insistent buzz of an alarm clock; often, they never quite lose that frantic pitch. You race to work, fighting highways and streets packed with cars and people. You miss your breakfast. Then, you spend the day wrestling with uncooperative computers, telephones, copiers, and fax machines. You run errands feverishly during your lunch hour and arrive late to meetings. Finally, you return home, exhausted by the day's events.

Peace is rare in our lives. Taking time to center ourselves or to think introspectively seems a luxury, one we can't always justify.

Instead, we race at a ridiculous pace, juggling the needs of career, family, and community. We forget that we need time and space to replenish our emotional resources. Without such opportunities for renewal, we begin to feel anxious and irritable, and eventually find that we must seek sanctuary from the world. For many of us, it is in the solitude and safety of a garden that we experience the deepest sense of peace. Here, we feel tranquil and centered, finally in control of life's pace.

A sanctuary garden is not just an attractive arrangement of plants, pathways, and sculpture. Rather, it is an environment we

choose to create as a personal refuge. In it, we tailor nature carefully to fit our human scale. From earliest history, gardens have implied enclosure, a separation of the garden from the other. By the very act of entering the garden, we can separate ourselves from our other lives. Surrounded by green, living things, we experience feelings of contentment, and we are able to find peace. After a few moments in a garden, the day's stresses and tensions lift—muscles feel lithe, nagging thoughts and worries retreat.

Physicians have documented peoples' reactions to nature, and found that they

LEFT: *A lengthy path from the street to the garden's entrance serves as a passage from the work-a-day world into the safety of the sanctuary.*
OPPOSITE: *An undulating carpet of vibrant green and gold spreads beneath a simple bench, and is punctuated by spiky foliage and a Japanese stone lantern.*

For many of us, it is in the solitude and safety of a garden

that we experience the deepest sense of peace.

experience reduced anger, diminished fear, and a more positive attitude when in a garden. Garden scents, sounds, colors, and textures have been shown to stimulate the release of relaxing hormones. As a result, we experience measurable physical and emotional changes: our immune systems improve, pain eases, and we are lifted spiritually. Our gardens quite literally heal us, restoring equilibrium to both our bodies and our minds.

As the pace of our lives continues to quicken, we need to assure that peaceful sanctuaries remain part of our world. We must learn the art of creating garden spaces devoted to peace and harmony. For not all gardens are peaceful. Some are filled with chaotic colors and bountiful shapes that animate us with their energy. Other spaces are shaded, moody, or dominated by historical or design themes. But a peaceful garden is intended solely to protect the visitor from the troubled world; disturbing colors, discordant sounds, and jarring accents must all be edited from this sanctuary space.

Creating a tranquil garden is like crafting a quilt. All the patches and threads must work together to achieve a total effect, one of comfort, serenity, and safety. Use sound, fragrance, color, and texture to create a soothing scene that will restore your spirit and bring you peace. The serenity of the space is determined by how well you are able to piece together the sensual elements. In a tranquil garden you want to feel at home, gently lulled into a state of relaxation.

Sound can be one of the most calming features of the sanctuary. When we think about a peaceful space we usually associate it with silence, but no garden is absent of sound, and the serene sanctuary is no exception. If you analyze the "quiet," you will discover that it is actually full of soft and subtle background noises. The key to sound in a peaceful garden is to arrange, as best you can, for pleasant, more or less constant notes:

RIGHT: *In a tranquil space, consider how a bench's color will contrast or harmonize with the garden and how its graceful lines can make a planting more special.* OPPOSITE: *This small pool offers a peaceful refuge beneath the limbs of a dwarf Japanese maple.*

places are characterized by freedom from agitation and disturbances. When crafting your peaceful sanctuary, do your best to filter out the bustle and noise of the outside world. Consider planting living screens—of evergreen or deciduous shrubs or trees—that muffle intruding clamor. Latticework trained with vines or climbers can also prove useful as a sound barrier. Walls and fences, too, offer refuge from the cacophonous world, filtering out visual "noise" as well.

The sound of water is a prized healing asset in the peaceful garden. Its presence is a physical reminder that it is a necessity of all life. Water symbolizes purity and rebirth,

build an elaborate pond or simply fill a shallow dish with water, the sound and motion of water stirs us inside.

Water also awakens the child within us. We are all drawn to explore the banks of a stream. We love the rushing motion of a creek in spring or the gentle lapping of waves against a lake's shore. Deep inside we long to revisit the innocence of youth—to touch the surface of a pond, searching the surface for fish, to explore its mossy, green banks. Playing with water puts us in touch with a simpler time, with a perhaps more peaceful self.

Another integral strand in the peaceful garden is the element of scent. Thousands of

Water symbolizes purity and rebirth,
its cleansing properties both literal and metaphorical.

singing birds in the tree limbs above, lazily humming insects, croaking frogs, trickling water. Human sounds, like the retreating footsteps of a neighbor or the rhythmic creak of a chair rocking on a wooden porch, can also be wonderfully familiar and calming. Sound, you see, need not distract you from feelings of respite, and in fact can enhance the peaceful atmosphere.

What we mean by quiet is the exclusion of unwanted sounds. Slamming doors, car horns, and strident voices destroy the restfulness of the sanctuary; our most peaceful

its cleansing properties both literal and metaphorical. The recycling, replenishing water of a fountain echoes the transformation and cycling in our own lives. In addition, the sound of running water is soothing to the soul, and masks unpleasant, intrusive noises. Even water described as still will show movement when the surface ripples with the wind or with the drop of a leaf. In the presence of water, we feel invigorated and strengthened by nature's resilience and beauty, even as the soft, quiet motion calms us. Whether you choose to

times a day we breathe in and we breathe out. Scents do not just waft across the air; they become a part of us, we literally draw them into our bodies. Vitally connected with memory, scents can connect us to moments when we felt safe and well cared for. Stock your garden with fragrances that trigger pleasant recollections; note that these scent memories are intensely personal, and will be different for each gardener.

Or scents may calm us with their magical chemistry: we respond automatically to the fresh, earthy smell of light spring rain

In the quiet of a tree–shaded backyard a bog garden thrives; yellow flag irises, variegated irises, Japanese candelabra primroses, and rhododendrons exist as swathes of color in the filtered light.

OPPOSITE: A small stream lined with layers of green adds a freshness that only water can bring. RIGHT: *Like a mirror set into the field, this pond reflects the placid farm land-scape—rhubarb, Siberian iris, and* Helictotrichon *frame the bank.*

as it covers the landscape with a silken mist; we relax when we catch a whiff of flower-perfumed air as it rises from a hot summer garden; we are healed with the release of a crushed herb's aroma; we are relieved as we inhale the dense chill of the deep shade. Even without knowing their exact composition, or perhaps because we cannot know it, the complicated perfumes of the garden help us transcend the cares of the day. In the garden we are removed from the stale and over—air conditioned or too-heated atmosphere of modern office buildings, malls,

and supermarkets, with their attendant pressures and demands. In the garden we don't dwell on financial worries or job security—we need only absorb the heady scent of the outdoors and we are reminded that there is another way of life. The redolence of the garden insists on our connectedness to nature and confirms our ultimate reliance on her resources.

As powerful as our sense of smell may be, it is nevertheless true that sight dominates our experience in the garden. Color has a profound effect on our spirits, and

when woven skillfully with light it can manipulate the mood of any space. In order to create an atmosphere of peace in our sanctuaries, we must consider color carefully, choosing a palette that inspires tranquillity rather than excitement.

While we often take the color green for granted, this soothing hue offers us a deep sense of comfort all year long. We associate green with nature's cycles; it is the emblem of new growth. Green also creates a tonal space between other colors, adding a sense of openness and visually calming the area it

In the presence of water, we feel invigorated and strengthened by nature's resilience and beauty, even as the **soft, quiet motion** calms us.

pervades. A carpet of grass balances the variations in flower colors and leaf contours. The primary healing color, green is more restful to the eye than any other in the spectrum. Stepping through an orchard, pasture, or meadow you experience this feeling of serenity firsthand.

White, the absence of color, signifies peace and purity of the soul. In the landscape, it represents stillness and allows the mind to come to rest. While white complements almost any color in the garden, it is also a popular choice for monochromatic theme gardens. Gardens made solely of white are magical, angelic, and ethereal. In the moonlight, white flowers reflect the ghostly beams, glowing like faint lanterns along the path. In daylight, white flora—like blank leaves of paper—do not require attentive study, they simply complement and accentuate the plants around them.

Pale pinks in the garden remind us of summer lipsticks; feminine and sweet, they erase hard edges. Shades of pink are comforting in their familiarity, inviting relaxation and softening colors around them. Visually blissful, pale pinks do not leap at or jar visitors. Perfect in groupings, blush-tinted flowers instill a tenderness and an innocence in the peaceful garden, pairing beautifully with whites, blues, lavenders, and greens.

Blue in the garden can be difficult to define; it has a tendency to mask other colors, so too much blue can be overwhelming. Add it carefully to your peaceful sanctuary's palette. But blue can also be very calming, and it is present in an endless variety of tones and tints, from the palest Scotch crocus to the deepest blue cornflower. But blue will also arrive in your garden in another form. In the waning light of dusk all objects are tinged with blue. Twilight is a peaceful time

LEFT: The landscape, dominated by soothing green, is enhanced by points of gleaming color. OPPOSITE: *There is perhaps nothing more calming than a freshly mown field bathed in early morning light. Changes in the light will transform the colors in your garden as the hours pass.*

We associate green with nature's cycles;

it is the emblem of new growth.

of day in the garden because colors are muted. Yielding to the failing light, every form is clothed in softness, bringing comfort and calm.

Violet is a special color in a peaceful sanctuary. Warm and welcoming, this hue envelopes you in its velvety folds. In the deepest stages of meditation, once the mind has emptied of all clutter, violet appears to fill the void. This meditative state is profoundly peaceful, and including violet in your flower palette will echo this aura in your garden.

Remember when combining colors that your ultimate goal is to create a space that soothes the soul, and that this means different things to different people. In general, though, a peaceful garden will not be filled with riotous color; instead, the tints are gentle and mild, dominated by healthy swathes of green foliage, mosses, and grasses.

Also consider, in a peaceful garden, how you'll combine other design features, such as patterns and textures. You do not want chaotic patterns or textures that work against one another. Generally, it is best to choose just one or two distinctive pattern

TOP LEFT: *Variegated Japanese hops* (Humulus japonicus 'Variegatus') *looks delicately painted.*
TOP RIGHT: *The pink-kissed miniature rose 'Child's Play' is an exquisite choice for the peaceful garden.* ABOVE: *A boldly painted seat remains a colorful accent year 'round.* OPPOSITE *Bleeding heart* (Dicentra spectabilis), *a graceful shade plant, has heart-shaped, pendant flowers that dance with the slightest breeze.*

LEFT: *Like green swords, iris foliage pushes up from the pond floor, thrusting toward the sky. Bergenia, Iris laevigata 'Variegata' and Acorus punctuates the banks of this meadow pond.* OPPOSITE: *Bridges, whether or not they span water, signify the crossing of a threshold or a step into new territory.*

or texture types and confine yourself to those. Remember that there are infinite subtle adornments in nature, and that these will keep your garden interesting even without showy statements.

Gardens are at their most calming to the eye when they are symmetrically designed, simple in shape and form. Lines must be organic and natural rather than artificially straight or jarringly angular in order for the space to feel comfortable. One way of achieving a harmonious balance in the garden is to adopt a simplified version of a Japanese philosophy. Japanese designers think of the materials in their gardens as possessing a gender: tall and linear objects embody masculine forces, while small, rounded forms represent feminine power.

All objects must be partnered—you wouldn't place a male in the garden without also adding a female. Positioning elements in this manner assures a balanced space that works as a harmonious whole.

We personalize our gardens with structures and accents, tailoring their design and details to help us achieve the peaceful effect we desire. A garden bridge leads us across the garden, transporting us to a quieter place by drawing a border between the peaceful space and outside havoc. A bridge symbolizes a journey, and provides a link, both physically and metaphorically, between two unlike things. From the bridge you might stand and watch your reflection in the water below or search for the movement of fish. You don't need water to incorporate a

bridge into your garden; the bridge can be used as a decoration or as a symbolic threshold. Gravel is sometimes used to represent water beneath a bridge, with carefully raked lines replicating the flow of water.

Thresholds are important to a peaceful garden because they define a passage from one state to another. As you cross the threshold, your gait slows, your shoulders, now unburdened by stress, lift. You clear your mind of intruding thoughts. As you step through a portal, your day melts away and you experience new-found peace. A stroll path, one that has a meandering pace and many twists and turns, lets you appreciate the beauty of the natural world that surrounds you. The green scenery works its charm, calming you with each step.

A striking red color, like the fish that dart beneath it, this Japanese bridge is the perfect spot to enjoy a slightly elevated view of the garden or to watch koi play at the surface of the water.

Fences, walls, or hedges announce the perimeters of our havens and preserve the symmetrical order of the space. Walls and fences may be constructed from any number of materials, including stone, brick, or wood, and, depending upon their height and design, may provide good places to gaze over or through. Serene views beyond the garden calm us, while inside the wall's boundaries we feel sheltered. Walls and fences also prevent unwanted interruptions and intrusions. Masked in green tendrils, fences are whimsical and relaxing, their linear form disguised by draping climbing vines. We are indeed enveloped in a private sanctuary.

Another garden structure with great possibilities for bringing peace is the arbor.

Wonderfully shady green caves, arbors create triumphal portals or, when placed against a wall or hedge, hidden recesses. The gentle, organic shape of an arbor is pleasing to the eye; its arching lines recall the magic of rainbows with their promise of gold reward.

There is also a range of larger structures that may reside in the peaceful garden. Greenhouses and lathe houses are protected outdoor rooms devoted to plants; there is nothing more sublime than a house built expressly for growing things. Surrounded by flowers and foliage, you are immediately calmed. Enveloped in an abundance of oxygen, you become giddy. The peace that comes after a few hours in a greenhouse is unparalleled. You can't be noisy in a growing house—it has the sacred quality of a

library. Listen only for the gentle creep of growing limbs.

Swinging, like the rock of a cradle, is an undeniably calming motion. Swings provide a charming, old-fashioned accent, as well as stunning views of your garden. As you glide to lofty heights through the whipping wind, your garden passes beneath you. The sky and clouds seem just an arm's reach away. The rhythmic movement lulls you, bringing daydreams. If swinging isn't your style, perhaps the gentle sway of a hammock will work the same magic.

Hammocks, horizontal versions of swings, allow us to recline in peaceful repose for hours. Requiring only two trees (or a hammock stand), a hammock immerses you in the garden. Its slow, even motion

You can't be noisy in a growing house—it has the sacred quality of a library.

Listen only for the gentle creep of growing limbs.

ABOVE: *A solitary swing beckons from its place within a vine-covered pergola.*
OPPOSITE: *Set within the embrace of four ginkgo trees, a collection of seats becomes an outdoor room for entertaining or for quiet evenings with family.*

induces napping. You can't lie in a hammock and be anything but relaxed. The net enfolds you like a butterfly in a cocoon. The web pattern pushes gently against your skin. A book tents on your chest. With each sway, creaks emanate from the ropes as they roll over ridges of bark.

But whatever else you have in your sanctuary, no peaceful garden is complete without seating. If you choose a hidden spot for your seat, it provides a great retreat. If you select a colored bench, it can accentuate and complement its surroundings. If you choose a naturalistic design, your seat will blend quietly with the environment. There is nothing like a comfortable garden seat to inspire you to collect your thoughts. Drag a chair to your favorite spot and breathe the fragrance of fresh cut grass and perfumed petals. Watch insects brazenly munch a leaf. Bask in the sun. Feel the sense of well being. Luxuriate in the serene beauty and quiet around you.

Seats also invite you to share your tranquility with others. We often feel that all is right with the world when we are in the company of friends and family. Relationships that comfort and nurture us bring us peace, and seats and benches allow us to share a moment or a meal with our dearest ones. Tucked into the garden, surrounded by loved ones and nature, evenings pass in utter contentment.

In the peaceful garden we seek an arrangement of colors, textures, scents, and sounds that calms and nourishes us, and we complement this overall design with objects that offer easeful pleasure.

Over and over again we return to the roots of our childhood, striving to re-create the careless days and purity of spirit we experienced in youth. One could claim that our gardens are simply adult substitutes for the

Relationships that comfort and nurture us bring us peace, and seats and benches allow us to share a moment or a meal with our dearest ones.

playgrounds of our childhood. There we spent hours pounding together forts and little houses, made of scrap planks and cartons. Afterward, we whiled away hours in these havens playing alone or in concert with friends, inventing games and patching together imaginary worlds. Maybe you squeezed yourself into a secret niche: a tiny spot all your own beneath a hedge or between the limbs of an immense shrub in your backyard. On the pressed-earth floor, you played and dreamed beneath the tangle of wooden

arms. And in these places you spent your first hours of tranquil daydreaming or quiet alone time. These were our first peaceful sanctuaries. We attempt to reconstruct these sacred places as adults in our own backyards. Relishing the peace and playful innocence of childhood, we create places with similar qualities in the hope of recapturing those feelings of supreme contentment.

Creating a peaceful sanctuary garden is just one step toward honoring a different vision of the world. If you are able to redis-

cover peace and balance within yourself while safe in your sanctuary, you can learn to carry those feelings with you outside. You will have created a place that is sacred, like a temple or a church. Our gardens help us maintain the delicate balance between the external demands of our lives and our interior emotional needs. They are places that heal us emotionally and physically. A peaceful sanctuary is truly a little paradise on this earth, the greatest refreshment that nature can offer humanity.

LEFT: *Meadows are perfect places to explore, ideal for stepping through grasses, searching for hidden wildflowers, or listening for the rustle of wayward breezes.*
OPPOSITE: *A gazebo—the word means, literally, "I shall see"—creates a place from which we can appreciate the peace of the garden.*

Relishing the peace and playful innocence of childhood,
we create places with similar qualities in the hope
of recapturing those feelings of supreme contentment.

CHAPTER TWO

CHANGE

Across the windowpanes creeps the shadow of a grayish brown branch that resembles a grandmother's beautiful, aged hands. Each granite-colored digit lifts awkwardly from dark, knotted, gnarled joints. As months tumble along, one after the other, the days shorten then lengthen again, the changing seasons measured by this silent, waving arm.

Outside the window, autumn brings flames of color to the tree, extending a foliage sunset from hours to weeks. It starts with a rich kimono red, gradually brightening to jack-o-lantern orange and then dulling to sweet cinnamon. The brittle leaves hang on the branch, ready to drop. Backlit by the sun, they look like ancient parchment maps, veins leading off toward new territories. Eventually, they fall, joining mountainous drifts of leaves lining the street. You inhale the sweet, moist, earthy perfume of decaying leaves and hear the musical crunch of curling dried leaves under pedestrians' feet. Like little winged packages, the samoras leap into the wind, each with a mission to sink into fertile soil.

Winter arrives, bringing Morse-code messages tapped by bark fingers on the pane. The gently creaking limbs moving with the wind edge nearer. Snow coats the branch with a fluffy white collar. Finally, tiny red bumps coat the smooth, gray bark. These are buds, ready to burst at the first sign of warmth.

Spring delivers needles of cold rain against the window. Creatures pass, busily making their way along the tree's branched highways. Little white spring flowers in discreet lines look like ladies' underthings dangling on a clothesline. Crinkly new leaves unfurl, shaped like fat green hands with triangles for fingers. So new and bright, the

LEFT: *Change, irrepressible and inevitable, is the catalyst for great beauty in the garden. Leaves of Japanese maple* (Acer palmatum) *smolder like hot coals, illuminating the autumn day.* OPPOSITE: *Snow coats surfaces with a pristine white layer, reversing silhouettes and revealing the garden's structure.*

We find solace in the permanence of nature.
But a garden's eternal character derives
from the very fact that it is always changing.

little leaflets appear almost neon. Electrical storms leave long, fuzzy, green filaments stuck to the screen.

In summer, the tree's foliage creates a moving green dome above and, looking up through its branches, skies appear dotted with green clouds. As you step to the window, the shaded outline of leaves patterns your skin, cooling your face and arms. Breezes, caught by leaf surfaces, are shuffled in; the curtains billow. No day is ever the same, even in a world as small as eight panes. This glass-framed limb reminds us that transformations

occur constantly and consistently everywhere we turn.

When you stand at the foot of a tree, your back resting against its sturdy trunk, you can feel the stability of this living thing. We find solace in the permanence of nature. But a garden's eternal character derives from the very fact that it is always changing. Nature operates in infinite circles, in a myriad of forms, gigantic to minuscule. Change takes many guises: the procession of the seasons, the unhurried growth of colorful lichen layers on a rock,

the gradual rounding of stones on a stream-bank, the metamorphosis of larva into moth or flower into fruit. Nature reminds us that we are always in a dynamic state, continually evolving. A thing that never changed would remain incomplete, eventually becoming a relic of a world that no longer existed.

We go to our gardens to seek solace, to refresh our spirits, and to remove ourselves from the chaos of the world. We look for comfort in the lush, green arms of our garden enclosures. In our everyday lives, we may accept change grudgingly. In the garden,

OPPOSITE: *These silken wisps of thread will catch shifting breezes, carry new seeds aloft, and set them in new earth, preserving the circle of seed to flower.*
LEFT: *Melodic and musical, moving water refreshes and sustains the changing landscape.*

Fences divide the world into manageable spaces and help define the shift of character from the world outside to the security of the enclosed place.

47

C
H
A
N
G
E

however, we nurture and celebrate its stunning beauty.

We note with pleasure the swollen flower bud that, petals still wrapped tightly in a colored cocoon, begins to unfurl its tissue-thin petals. We wait impatiently for the new flower. As trees don their funeral robes in crimson, cayenne, mustard, and paprika, we cherish the passing season, searching for excuses to take long walks. Snow wipes the landscape clean, returning it to natal innocence; we hesitate to mar the fresh surface with footsteps, but can't resist the blank canvas and add our own patterns to the mix.

Hurrying change, we place spring-blooming bulbs and trees near paths, anxiously awaiting the first flush of color. Spring petals drop, rolling fragrant pink carpets across the bare ground.

We delight in the mutability of the garden because there we have learned to accentuate the processes of nature. We plan our gardens so as to view more closely the changes of the world, selecting plants specifically for their bold autumn foliage, their especially profuse blooms, their bright winter berries. A garden is thus the organization of change, and gardening is a con-

tinual process of observing, considering, making changes, and observing again. A cycling landscape allows us to appreciate beauty in all its variety, to discover a treasure in every form.

Time pushes us all toward uniqueness of character, but in the garden we do not dwell on youth. We welcome wide girths and thick trunks. We enjoy stooped and twisted limbs. Trees, contorted and shaped by the elements, are cherished. These unique shapes become focal points, and in turn emphasize the plant community around them. True gardeners do not favor any part of the cycle.

RIGHT: *Crisp, green leaves unfold, awkward and gangly as adolescents, reminding us that change is not always graceful.* OPPOSITE, LEFT: *Nature is not intimidated by diversity or variety. As illustrated by this intricate artichoke plant, nature adeptly embraces a vast array of beauty, every shape and size imagined.* OPPOSITE, RIGHT: *Russet, salmon, and magenta— a profusion of colors in this bougainvillea are revealed by the shifting light of day.*

In our everyday lives, we may accept change grudgingly. In the garden, however, we nurture and celebrate its stunning beauty.

They delight in the beige, brown, and fading skeletons of a season's end just as they welcome the brightness of new blooms.

No single aspect of a garden is a representative of change—instead, change can be found in every detail. Look carefully for signs of transformation. Remember your own metamorphoses, from babyhood on. Finding a way to incorporate your own life changes into your garden helps you create a space that reflects your personal experiences as well as all life's journeys. You might wish to include that special flower your grandmother so loved, or you may plant a garden of the blooms used in your wedding bouquet; perhaps you'll plant a tree for each child born to you or cultivate a flowering vine that grew near the first home you owned. Commemorate your past in your garden, and you will have carved a spot that will support you, nurture you, and help you celebrate your own continuing growth.

All gardens remind us that we are part of a larger universe, where nothing has a permanent identity. All things are made of constituent elements, the parts interdependent. Just as people rely on their communities to usher them through life's difficulties and celebrate its achievements, plant and creature communities rely on each other for reproduction and continuity. Each layer in a landscape—from the tree canopy above to ground-loving herbaceous plants—is interwoven. The fragrances and colors of neighboring flowers attract insects needed for pollination. Fruit and seeds summon wildlife, and the animals then carry them to fertile soil, preserving and redistributing the plants' populations. Trees provide shade and shelter from weather conditions, while the plants below protect the soil by preventing erosion and preserving moisture. In death,

RIGHT: *Mysterious and unhurried, the saffron yellow tips of this iris bud are the only hint of what lies furled within.*

OPPOSITE: *Like panes in a stained glass window, autumn leaves filter and color the light in this stand of birches.*

OPPOSITE: *The dusty, faded skeleton of this zinnia, still lovely as it withers, reminds us that beauty is found even in the shadow of death.* RIGHT: *Resembling sugared pastilles, beech leaves caught unexpectedly by winter dangle like glazed treats.*

plants return organic material and nutrients to the soil to be recycled by the surrounding plant community.

In observing and accepting change in the garden we reconcile with the idea of change in our own lives. We can better face the darkness and sorrow when we know that, if we have patience, we will emerge into a new spring. We must simply have faith in the rhythms of change: the gifts of life are inevitably followed by loss, which is just as inevitably followed by renewal. Watch as the circles of life inscribe themselves across your garden and learn to recognize their subtle signs.

Sounds give clues of impending change: whispers on the wind announce alterations. Ice weights leaves and limbs, causing them to rub against one another and send delicate tinkling noises across the landscape. Listen for the joyful jump and run of springwater as it gushes over, under, and around stones; the quiet hum of water as it disappears under a sheet of ice only to resurface in deeper waters; the tick-tock of icicles melt-ing, drops running the length of the frozen wand before falling into the void and smack-ing on the first hard surface; the musical notes of birds as they call back and forth. These are the sounds you must seek, and if you listen carefully you will find that the garden provides a soulful orchestra.

Once your senses have become attuned to the rhythm of this humming cycle, you can experience change in every object, in every cell, with every sense. Invite the sounds of change into your garden by incorporating

We must simply have faith in the rhythms of change:
the gifts of life are inevitably followed by loss,
which is just as inevitably followed by renewal.

Color is the calling card of the natural world—
every change is announced with a new tint.

water into your design and by tailoring your plant list. Even a small stream, fountain, or pool will allow you to appreciate the material shift from the tepid waters of deep summer to the crackling ice of January to the clear, cold flow of spring. Plants that retain their architectural shape throughout the winter—trees, shrubs, tall grasses, and so on—will become outlined in ice during freezing rains, slowly dripping away this frozen mantle as the spring thaw commences.

Fragrance in a changing landscape is often less about an actual perfume and

more about an aura of sensuality. Every living thing has a specific scent, its own shadow of fragrance. The natural world communicates through these olfactory drifts. Flowers exude seductive fragrances that draw pollinators near. Creatures release pheromones and scents that warn, signal, and attract. Humans have a less perceptive sense of smell than some of our fellow animals, but we, too, luxuriate in the perfume of transformation.

Decaying plants fill the crisp autumn air with dank scents that tingle our nostrils.

Winter has a clean, stinging, animal scent, like wet wool. It reddens the tip of your nose and clears your head. Spring rolls back the snow and releases the rich smell of covered soil and skunk cabbage: malodorous, musky, rich. Manure, mixed with the delicate sweetness of newly opened leaves and fragrant flowers, broadcasts its fragrance across beds, reminding us that the growing season is beginning anew. Summer smells are pure and undiluted. Strong and heady, they are of sunburning petals and approaching rainstorms.

Color, however, is less subtle an element of the changeable sanctuary. We live immersed in the buoyant world of light and color, and everything we experience has its signature tone or hue. Color is the calling card of the natural world—every change is announced with a new tint. Bursting buds are pink with infancy, but soon reach a rich mature color, then fade gradually, edges browning before they fold. Fruit arrives green, but attractive rosy hues signal ripeness. Before long, a creature will swoop down to pluck and eat it, thankful for the colorful reminder.

New leaves are radiant against the conservative drab hues of winter. Summer colors sizzle with high temperatures. Plants absorb the strong light and heat, splashing it across every leaf and blade. Autumn colors, like lanterns about to be extinguished, have just a hint of encroaching darkness. Winter grays and browns soak up every last bit of cold sunlight. Light reflected and refracted by starched white snow speeds across every surface, ricocheting sharply, dilating your pupils.

Light plays a leading role in a cycling landscape, transforming it daily. The

changing scene is controlled by the direction of the sun's rays, its personality and energy morphing in the shifting light. Spring days linger, prompting growth and fresh bloom. When summer comes, days are long and intense. We become extroverts, soaking up every bit of sun and life we can. Autumn brings an end to the intense light and energy, and we prepare for darker days. We draw inward, becoming more introspective. Winter is a time of failing light, a time to rest and contemplate.

Arrange your garden so that you can appreciate the play of light and shadow

ABOVE: *Money plant* (Lunaria), *tucked amidst 'Clara Curtis' chrysanthemums, reflects silvery moons of light.* OPPOSITE, LEFT
AND RIGHT: *Pink and cream foxgloves* (Digitalis spp.) *rise from a sea of verdant leaves like church steeples above a village. Months later,*
the same garden pulses with lipstick reds, dense greens, and golds; pale spring blooms are replaced with passionate summer color.

A rosebud waits for a signal to unfurl. Each petal of the 'Evelyn' rose, one of David Austin's English roses, gradually blanches to a confectionery pastel.

LEFT: *Nestled beside a narrow pool, feathery astilbes accentuate and soften the stark rock, creating a miniature oasis.*
OPPOSITE, TOP: *Soft and yielding to the touch, water also possesses great strength, able to reshape or wear away the most resistant of surfaces.*
OPPOSITE, BOTTOM: *Obscure at first, a hair-thin fissure will crawl across a rock's surface. Over time, the crevice's edges are pushed apart by the elements.*

throughout the seasons and at different times of day. Place benches strategically to take advantage of the morning or afternoon light, or site a seat in the dappled shade of a venerable tree.

Remember, too, that twilight—that shadowy border between day and night—is a magical time in the garden. It is also the daily interval when working people are most likely to spend time in the garden. Be sure to include some evening bloomers, such as angel's trumpet, night-flowering jessamine, four o'clocks, evening primroses, night phlox, and, of course, moonflowers. These secretive flowers, so unassuming by day and utterly vivacious at night, remind us of the entire nocturnal world with which we share the earth, and underline the transformation from day to night.

Shape, size, and structure also undergo incredible transformations. Trees start as tiny seedlings. Acquiring height, they lengthen and spread their limbs, reaching toward the sky. Smaller shapes echo this metamorphosis: egg sacks hang in dark corners until little wormlike creatures emerge. Gorging themselves, hardly able to move, they roll from one leaf banquet to the next. Sufficiently fattened, they wrap themselves in quiet and alter their shapes for flight.

Stones, a symbol of resistance, are subject to the transformation process as well, but their changes are generally so slow as to be imperceptible to us. Pushed to the earth's surface from its core by inner rumblings, stones are mammoth at first but are slowly whittled by the elements. They wear the history of this journey on their sur-

faces: colorful striations, gouged dimples, and deep cracks. Nature uses these footholds to wear down and eventually transform the rock's once-solid surface into the millions of little granules found in each handful of soil. Because they are so slow to change, stones represent permanence to us. Adding some large and beautiful stones to your garden will highlight dramatic contrasts with the more fleeting aspects of nature.

Plant textures and patterns also shift constantly, like a tapestry woven across the seasons. Every species and genus handles the stages of its own metamorphosis differently. Just as humans balance change and pressure in an endless variety of ways, plants lace together a myriad of forms and designs across the garden as time goes by. Some add

Stones, a symbol of resistance,
are subject to transformation processes as well,
but their changes are generally so slow
as to be imperceptible to us.

Just as humans balance **change** and pressure in
an endless variety of ways, plants lace together a myriad of
forms and designs across the garden as time goes by.

bright-colored berries. Others bring vivid washes of flowers or seedheads that move with the wind. Closer inspection allows you to trace the outline of leaves, peer into the intricate architecture of the stems and canopies. You'll see that little hairs dot the surface of the leaf and that thorns adorn stem lengths. Fruit and leaves seem to ripple outward with changing textures. They come from closed, centered points, gradually unfolding. Drifts of purple, blue, red, and pink glide across the petal surfaces like ripples in a pond, radiating outward. Pointed leaf ends lift and depress in infinite patterns and textures. Your eyes move across the landscape. Capture it now, for when you return it will be changed.

To realize our greatest potential, we must embrace change without hesitation. Learn from the garden, which puts forth buds when offered only the suggestion of warmth, then, with courage, moves forward to flower.

ABOVE: *As delicately wrought as the finest painting, the gradations of color on the petals of 'John Warren' clematis beguile you with beauty.* RIGHT: *A Lenten rose* (Helleborus orientalis) *struggles in a late winter snow— change can set us upon a new course.*

CHAPTER THREE

PASSION

Roam this fertile red sea. Spreads of vivid burgundies, striking magentas, and glowing oranges touch pink-edged foam, reaching for green sands. The waves here—formed from earth, foliage, petals, and stems—are thick with texture; they curve and swell and fold. These waves roll with the buzz of bees and the layered sound of songbirds. Bright sunlight urges you on, moves you firmly forward. Your very being, awakened to air, scent, and color, is stirred to action. Before your mind can begin to speculate on your surroundings, your body has responded to the energy of the place.

In this sea made not of water but of plants, the flowers, trees, and vines are tucked lovingly into the earth's surface, fragrant and colorful, textured and delicious. This sea calls out to all life forms, you among them, to breathe in its plenty. Instinctively, you realize you have entered a passionate landscape, a garden designed to evoke the feelings residing deep within you. You join with the garden creatures, who survive in beauty and simplicity, adjusting to and using the environment about them to sustain and enrich their lives. Sensing the fragrance of life-in-action, you are held

in stunning observation of this lush and fertile world.

Perhaps what is most unique about a sanctuary garden designed to provoke human passion is its complete outward abundance, its interdependent glory. To feel the depths of passion stirring within us, our senses must be excited, overloaded. In such spaces, we ask ourselves, "Where does my passion come from? Why do I crave the tactility of this landscape, a landscape that enlivens me physically?" An answer: in this sort of garden we can revert to our most primal selves. In this space we are not cast inward, but rather

LEFT: *Red, pink, and coral-colored azaleas spread like waves rounding a shoreline. The wide-arching spread of color surrounding the bench stimulates vital senses.*
OPPOSITE: *A flowering crabapple exudes happiness and hope. Here, delicate pink flowers dance together on limbs, reminding us of care-free times.*

Perhaps what is most unique about a sanctuary

garden designed to provoke human passion

is its complete outward abundance, its interdependent glory.

68

*The sun's heat and vitality
illuminate the tender-layered
tissue of this rich red-orange
poppy, adding to the delicate
sensuality of the passionate
garden.*

far-reaching spectrum and fix on the hottest colors. These colors rivet your attention, immersing you in emotion and carrying you along in rivers of brilliance.

Red has been called the color of anger and warning, of change and revolution—it is the color of fire and of blood. As the color of our vital fluid, it is thus a powerful reminder of life. Considered the most forward of colors in the garden, red does indeed hold a magnificent strength, and demands action like no other color. All shades and tones of red remain true to this profile.

Pink, a close sibling of red, evokes an altogether different response. Pinks also live in the garden of passion, but they represent a delicate sensuality, a quiet innocence. Sister hues (pale rose, bright magenta) coax gentleness from the gruffest among us. Pale pink tones, complemented with white and silver or brightened with red and green, induce a sense of calm, asking little of the eye and soothing the spirit. Bright pinks, on the other hand, shock us. Magenta in the garden fairly hollers, aching for attention.

outward to the forces and potential of the greatest of all gifts: life.

In a garden of passion, the vital senses—sight, smell, touch, sound—must be roused, and done so luxuriously. To fulfill the incipient promise of energy and excitement, the variable strands of color, sound, texture, fragrance, and pattern must be woven together gracefully. When these elements are well married, our senses, one by one, are truly captivated by the garden.

Often, it is color that touches us first in a passionate garden sanctuary. Colors are actually created by different wavelengths of light that are absorbed and reflected at different rates by flowers, leaves, blades of grass. Thus, color and light can be consid-

ered in tandem. A key element in the passionate garden is bright sunlight—the light is not diffused through trees, nor is it kept in hiding behind a tree's canopy. Because we associate passion with brightness, the sun must be allowed to visit openly this life-affirming space. Shadows are few, and dark hollows are illuminated with beaming color.

Imagine yourself in a room of blue, of white, of peach. Each color evokes a different emotional response, a phenomenon used with purpose by designers to create spaces that elicit feelings of calm or excitement, contentment or joy. So it is in a garden "room." Our earth displays millions of hues and shades and tones, but in a passionate landscape we limit our use of this

Considered the most forward of colors in the garden,

red does indeed hold a magnificent strength,

and demands action like no other color.

LEFT: *The softly elusive scent of lilacs (Syringa vulgaris 'Paul Thirion') woos garden travelers from the path. The familiar fragrance and subtle color sym-bolize spring.* TOP: *Full blossoms spring from tightly held buds in this dazzling 'West Elkton' peony.* ABOVE: *The magenta of this rare Mexican vine, Delchampia, virtually screams for attention.*

Yellow and purple also have their place in a passionate landscape. Combined or apart, each has sensual affiliations of its own. Purple conjures images of luxurious wealth, storybook royalty, and romantic half-moon nights. Yellow speaks of hope, cheer, and the promise of spring. Reminding us of the sun's life-giving heat, yellow warms our bones, stirring us to move.

In passionate spaces, combinations of these intense colors create striking tints and riotous splashes. We stand in awe at the divine palette of nature. And then, once we have absorbed the kaleidoscope of color, our restless selves intuitively make room for the next sensual opportunity.

Sound in the garden results from both the types of plantings and the elements pre-sent. Like a composer, a gardener can orchestrate the sound of the garden, planting the "notes" to elicit musical responses from the vast world of insects and animals, as well as from other sources such as water or wind chimes. Even the rustle of grasses, the rattle of dried seedpods, and the swishing of leafy boughs stirring in the wind contribute to the complex harmonies of the garden.

ABOVE, LEFT AND RIGHT:
Color and exuberant texture
combine in star-of-Persia
(Allium christophii) *and*
Ammi visnaga *'Green Mist'.*
RIGHT: *Golden grasses and*
fragrant lavender explode like
fireworks in the landscape.
OPPOSITE: *Saturated color*
and ripples of seersucker-like
texture draw the eye to
'Johnson's Blue' geranium.

Like a composer, a gardener can orchestrate the sound of the garden, planting the "notes" to elicit musical responses from the vast world of insects and and animals, as well as from other sources such as water or wind chimes.

Though we have learned to cast environmental sounds to the back of our minds, hearing is a blessed gift. With just a bit of thought and practice, we can easily sharpen our ability to absorb desirable sounds. Close your eyes for a moment and count the sounds you hear now. Do you hear just one? Or, if you listen more acutely, do you find that there are five, ten, or more sounds? What is the character of the sound in your space? Is it the whiz of a hundred cars rushing past your window or the sound of crickets rubbing their wings together? Can you make out both?

Sounds of nature can be overwhelming—a shrieking wind, an unsettling crack of thunder, waves crashing frightfully close to your back porch. More commonly, however, natural sounds are pleasing—hot-summer cicada raspings, the cricket chirps of a peaceful twilight, the hopeful songs of birds.

Within a passionate garden you should feel enveloped by a chorus of voices. Analyze the sound of the garden; locate the buzzing chords. Realize that the subtle energy of sound is more apparent when you enter the microscopic world of a bee who climbs within a flower. Observe as it attaches itself to a powdery stamen. Linger a moment and you'll discover that the bee has unimagined strength and fury. Vibrating the flower with its humming wings, the frenzied bee alights briefly to gather the luscious pollen coating the stamen. Such sounds help to create the energizing atmosphere of the passionate garden, they are the dramatic music of nature's onward battle.

Collect sounds in your garden by providing resources for the creatures who make them. Bluebirds, bobolinks, cardinals, chickadees, doves, and others birds must feel safe and protected, so make sure to include trees, shrubs, and dense plantings where they can take refuge from predators. Toads, praying mantises, crickets, cicadas, snakes, and other animal visitors will likewise appreciate a safe haven; wild-inspired plantings such as wildflower meadows and stands of tall grasses will encourage a cacophony of trills, chirrups, croaks, and twitters in the garden.

Powdery stamens emerging from an Oriental lily (Lilium 'Black Beauty') tantalize bees and other insects, helping to bring sound into the garden. The stamens' long, graceful form makes a perfect landing spot for buzzing insects.

To further welcome this rush and roar of life, spread a tantalizing banquet by including plenty of fruits, berries, and seed-producing plants, such as sunflowers, zinnias, amaranths, elderberries, viburnums, and so on. Birds and little animals will feast upon these garden delights. And remember that beneath your feet live insects, caterpillars, worms, and slugs, flourishing in fertile soil.

The sound of water, too, may denote energy—it contributes to the resounding whir in a passionate garden as it cascades, splashes, or gurgles. We recognize water sounds—whether pattering as rain, coursing down a human-made waterfall, or streaming from a bamboo faucet—as sounds of renewal and nourishment. Moving quickly, water generates excitement; dripping slowly it suggests

contemplation. Filling a quiet pool, it hints at reflection and repose.

Water has been an integral part of ancient religious and healing philosophies all over the globe for centuries. In Christian tradition, baptism with water symbolizes the cleansing of the soul by removing the stain of original sin, making the baptized eligible for salvation. Japanese gardeners provide stone basins that fill with water from a bamboo cane; a dipper invites vistors to rinse their hands in symbolic cleansing. Native Americans, too, treasure water. In celebrations for fertility or to break droughts, ritual dances honor water's life-giving properties. Instinctively, we know that water heals, refreshes, and nourishes. And water is an integral part of our own cellular makeup; indeed, it is an

essential component of all life. Its sound is acutely familiar, deeply meaningful.

Use water in your garden to set a mood: if you wish to rouse emotions, you may want to plan for sounds that invigorate you. For some, this means water that is splashing noisily, rushing and shouting. For others, a slow dripping, a single stream, or even a still pool may do the trick. Keep in mind that water is the playground of many creatures. Invite them into your space, to drink, to play, and to share in the sense of sanctuary.

Not only does water provide sensuous sound, it also offers a most tangible and necessary element for a passionate garden—texture. Texture suggests depth. It completes color and sound by bringing a wholeness, a richness, a third dimension to plants. Our

We recognize water sounds—whether pattering as rain, coursing down
a human-made waterfall, or streaming from a bamboo faucet—
as sounds of renewal and nourishment.

desire to touch fibrous leaves, rough bark, silky petals, and smooth stems is undeniable. Hands and fingers reach out to explore surfaces. Our skin begs for more information. We relate to the world around us through our sense of touch. Our interaction with nature becomes deeper and more intimate given the element of texture.

As an expression of texture in the garden, water has a special quality. It illustrates complete nourishment for whatever it is near. Its crystal drops shimmering upon a petal, a stem, or a leaf assure growth. How tempting are the tiny drops of water to our tongues on a hot day. And how fascinating it is to watch raindrops (or hose water) pelt a delicate leaf and cling in perfect symmetry upon the plant. Even without sipping the delicious beads, we can imagine the feel of cool liquid sliding onto our lips and tongues.

Rain, along with dew and other precipitation, provides natural water flow. Heavy rain accompanied by black clouds can darken a garden quickly, and dampens its atmosphere as well. A light rain, on the other hand, can lift the mood in the passionate garden. Raindrops drench limbs and stems, bending them with watery weight. Leaves respond to falling rain by bouncing and moving, and flowers gather rainwater to create pools of their own.

A brisk shower or an arching fountain gives life to sculptures, insinuating softness and movement. Hard surfaces coated with water shine, sparkle, and breathe. With the addition of water, handmade forms achieve new depth. Carved skirts billow in the wind; stone feet run for shelter.

As the first droplets descend, creatures peep and scurry, then fall silent in anticipation of the changes rain will bring. It may reorganize their landscape: branches might fall, grasses may be flattened, burrows could flood, the earth will undoubtedly become darker and muddier. When the drenching

ABOVE: *Transparent droplets ensure that the age-old beauty of the rose will live on.* BELOW: *Water, providing sensuous sound, texture, and movement in a garden, has a lovely way of bringing life even to inanimate objects.* OPPOSITE: *A rosebud, petals tightly bound in green leaves, is just hours away from full blossom. Soon enough, hidden petals will lose their shyness and join emboldened nature.*

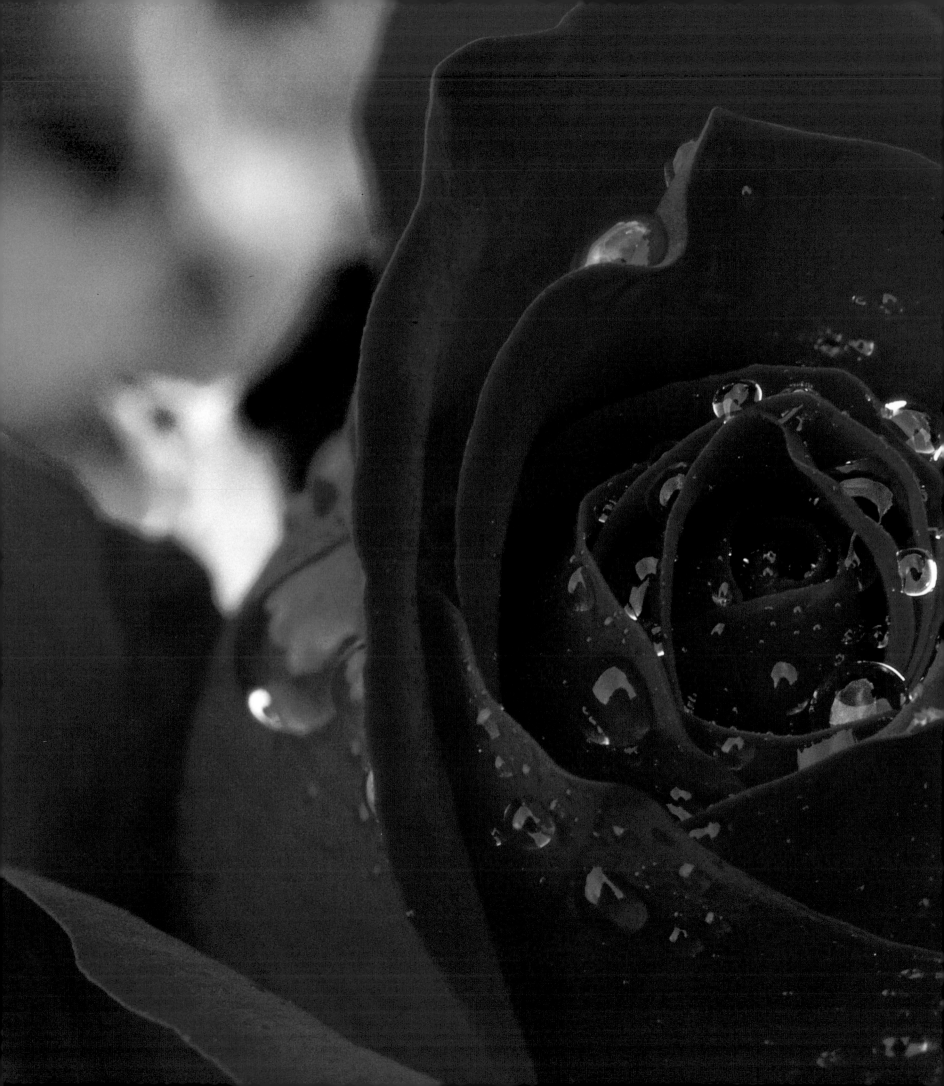

Tempting raindrops alight
upon the luscious red rose.
What better way to illustrate
water's depth and plenitude
than to join it with the cav-
ernous and heady petals of
this mature flower.

From the long-lasting and protective surface of a tree, to the **delicate** microstructure of the lily—with its sharp spears and powdery stamens—nature reveals her capacity for endless creativity.

draws to an end, the little animals reappear, busy and gleeful to be using this new element to their advantage.

Texture ornaments all corners of the garden, not only the places where water swirls. The plants themselves provide intricate forms and wondrous layers. Nature creates silky, scaled, furry, smooth, wet, and popping surfaces, to name just a few in her tactile scheme. Textures change from season to season, from tight, smooth bud to satiny flower and on to brittle skeleton.

Defined by surface patterns, textures compel us to explore the world around us through touch. From the long-lasting and protective surface of a tree, its bark rough and solid, to the delicate microstructure of the lily—with its sharp spears and powdery stamens—nature reveals her capacity for endless creativity.

Surface texture may be the first to appeal to us, mesmerizing us with its diverse and ardent patterns. But soon enough, the miraculous architecture of plants will capture

our attention as well: the reaching arms of a beech tree, the protective enclosure of a rose bush, the tropical insinuation of an immense fern. Here, texture is produced by layering. To create a layered garden, make sure to include varying heights and forms. Place the tallest plants toward the back and edges of the space; medium-height species fill middle ground, while low-growing plants are placed in the foreground. Such layering, particularly in trees and shrubs, expands the depth of textures. By twisting our bodies into the hidden

ABOVE: *Evergreen branchlets on a great Norway spruce* (Picea abies) *weep with majestic energy, creating layered shelter and prickly texture.* RIGHT: *With its bright orange center,* Helichrysum 'Silverbush' *unfurls with quiet allure.* OPPOSITE: *Snow resting softly along the wavy, gnarled branches of contorted hazel* (Corylus avellana 'Contorta') *reveals winter's cool romance.*

world behind the natural curtain or peeping through the hanging limbs, we become part of nature's brilliant engineering.

The elaborately sculpted reproductive systems of plants encourage a multitude of creative images and celebrate the fecundity of the natural world. Many artists look to nature's organic and erotic forms to inspire their own work; they imitate and recreate the rich, abundant, intricate structures. From each plant's texture, whether simple or com-

plex, we see the myriad of options Mother Nature offers us. From these structures we learn to value complexity and to respect the earth's profound beauty.

When speaking of passion in the garden, we cannot forget that progeny of desire, fruit. This most ancient symbol for passion, indulgence, and life brings even greater excitement to the landscape. Ripe fruit—a wondrous combination of texture, color, and architecture—symbolizes repro-

duction, the result of nature's dynamic workings. Fruit offers a temptation we can't refuse. When we see a peach, an orange, or a pear hanging from a tree, swollen with sweetness, bursting with juice, we recognize intuitively the treasure of its luscious interior. The sight and taste of fruits, resplendent with sugars, awakens a buried sensuality, for these jewels of nature have long been linked with eroticism and fulfillment of desire.

OPPOSITE: *Oranges, ripe and heavy with juice, fall from limb to ground in an expression of tantalizing temptation.* RIGHT: *Vivid pinks partnered with white in this 'Red Jade' crabapple blossom energize our souls. From petal to bud and from leaf to petiole, each portion illustrates nature's fine artistry.*

The sight and taste of fruits, resplendent with sugars, awakens a buried sensuality, for these jewels of nature have long been linked with fulfillment of desire.

While the scent of fruit stirs, the heady fragrance of earth, foliage, and flowers likewise engages the visitor in the passionate garden. In this space, you cannot escape the glorious aromas; the plants virtually demand an olfactory response. Inhaling the sweet and spicy scents invites deep breathing; surrounded by natural perfumes, your mind races with memories of bouquets long gone as you revel in the fragrant air.

Blooms with dizzying scents add much to the sanctuary in which passion rules: consider old garden roses, peonies, hyacinths, alyssum, lilacs, or fruit trees to name a few.

Neither delicate nor elusive, the scents of these flowers travel fleetly to your nose, leaving you giddy with pleasure and imploring you to bow and bend into their petals. Other flowers, such as violets and wildflowers, carry perfumes far more evasive. These tricksters woo you from your path with a hint of fragrance that disappears as you chase it, inviting you to search for the source.

A way to repay the garden's generosity is to join with it in movement. Walk, skip, run, jump. In a passionate garden, organic shapes create a landscape that encourages participation. Through the flowing lines of

the garden, we recall our own evolving forms and reconnect with our bodies. We often forget that our own human shapes are much like the forms we seek in the garden—the graceful limbs of trees and shrubs, sinuous pathways, and the gentle orbs of fruits and buds have resonance for us because we are well acquainted with the similar curves, swells, and rounded forms of our own bodies. Repeat these dynamic contours in the garden, and the resulting sanctuary calls to its visitors to celebrate their common forms. A serpentine plant bed sweeping down a slope invites you to blissfully roam its length. A splashing waterfall

Through the flowing lines of the garden,
we recall our own evolving forms and reconnect with our bodies.

asks for your hand beneath its cooling tumble. And, as in the human body, the bones of a garden are integral: vertical forms like trees, garden structures, and statuary should punctuate the view, endowing the garden with soaring height and a long-lasting frame.

The passionate garden, pulsing with activity, is open and airy. Few obstacles obstruct paths and energy circulates with ease. Unencumbered by walls and fences, a sprawling landscape releases you from oppressive confines. Passion here has ample room to grow.

To experience a passionate garden is to celebrate aspects of our humanness that are necessary to our survival: hope, joy, desire, surprise, and even anger. These types of sanctuary spaces remind us that we are a part of nature's dynamic whole, and without them we run the risk of losing touch with our essential selves. The passionate garden exists as a stage upon which we can symbolically display our deepest emotions, thus maintaining balance in our lives. You need not, however, play elaborate theatrical tricks to produce dramatic effects. In this bright, pulsing world the truths of the natural universe reign supreme. Design your sanctuary with the purpose of exalting the shapes and patterns of nature, and you will have a garden alive with feeling.

ABOVE: *Nature's forms, graceful, round, curving, upright, or stiff, bear a resemblance to human figures. Lay a path to emphasize such organic shapes—and to keep you moving.* OPPOSITE: *An azalea's fuchsia petals, so demanding in their brightness, set off a sculpted female figure, destined to play forever within the fertile grounds of a passionate garden.*

MYSTERY

We exist in a familiar world—for the most part. Stepping with care, we do our best to keep to the well-trodden path, though along it, invariably, sit obstacles, detours, and decisions. Beyond this oft-traveled trail there exists another world: the world of mystery. At times, we long to venture from our familiar way, to feel the thrill of adventure, to awaken to all the possibilities of life. With curiosity we peer into the depths of the dangerous forest, our feet still fixed firmly to the path. Sometimes curiosity overwhelms us and we set off on risk's byway, pursuing and probing mystery's offerings. Having the courage and determination to explore adds much to our perceptions about reality and life. Embrace the unfamiliar rather than avoiding it; we must participate in new adventures to grow and fulfill our potential.

Arranging our gardens to celebrate the unexpected is one way to welcome a sense of mystery into our lives: a turn of the path, a shadowy grove, or a cryptic stone tablet can all lend the garden an air of the extraordinary. Here we can create the secret garden we dreamed of in our youths, an enchanted place of magic, where anything is possible.

In a garden setting, an atmosphere of pervasive mystery finds an easy home. Left to grow according to their own natures, plants create enclosures—a tangle of vines, a bower of wild roses, a dense thicket of shrubs, a copse of trees. These types of wild but intimate spaces invite us to believe that they have been sought by no human before us. Encourage your plants to grow in these encircling formations (don't be afraid to lend a hand with judicious pruning and training—even the most untamed-looking landscapes are often the handiwork of an expert gardener). Create in your garden a spot with the aura of an undiscovered hideaway, and you automatically imbue it with a sense of mystery, while fashioning a miniature sanctuary.

An air of intrigue surrounds even the design and ornament of the mysterious sanctuary. Mazes, for example, have long delighted adventuresome visitors to the garden. Lost within the walls of a living puzzle, we seek to unlock its logic and find its secret heart. While few gardeners have the resources to design and maintain a full-sized maze, these growing conundrums can be

readily enjoyed at many public gardens. Some gardeners look to a fast-growing, less permanent alternative to the traditional evergreen shrubbery—one such idea is to create a maze of maize. Satisfyingly enigmatic, a corn maze offers a chance to wander intricate pathways, within hearing distance of other people yet far from a simple conclusion.

Other garden ornaments, too, aid the goal of adding mystery to the garden, and have the advantage of being more manageable than a maze. Time-worn statuary and weathered urns of ancient design suggest civilizations long dead, their secrets waiting to be uncovered. Our observations that gardens grow

Lost within the walls of a living puzzle,

we seek to unlock its logic and find its secret heart.

OPPOSITE: *The trademark of any mysterious garden, a beckoning, sun-dappled path urges one forward toward unknown outcomes.* ABOVE: *The curtain of branches from* Cedrus atlantica 'Glauca Pendula' *creates an almost-hidden retreat.* LEFT: *Gentle greens slide across the landscape, darkening surfaces here and there. Hidden structures pique our curiosity, alerting us to undiscovered hideaways.*

A corn maze, shown here with rich autumn reds,
golds, and greens, has more than a touch of mystery. Lost in
the repeating pathways of corn plants, this maze is a perfect
conundrum for a mystery garden seeker. Blood red
illuminated by yellow veins on the transforming corn leaf
reflects the season's striking changes.

ceaselessly, cycle to cycle, bring thoughts of what may one day be, as well as what might once have been. Enveloped in the quiet, shadowy world of the mysterious garden, we indulge our spirit of inquisitiveness. The garden of mystery attracts us because it grants us a rare opportunity to become adventurers; it offers us a chance to appease our restless souls. In this sanctuary we may shed our cautious, everyday selves and retreat into the playful explorations of childhood: comfort comes with the freedom to seek new and unexpected things. Here we are poised to discover new aspects of our personalities and to glory in traits normally stifled by responsibilities. This landscape captures us and holds us in its grip, freeing us from judgment and expectation. Here, indeed, grows a sanctuary garden where we can celebrate the secrets of the world around us.

In haunting combinations, light, sound, fragrance, color, and texture weave mystery's veil. Murky light filtering through tree limbs looming like guards overhead creates a surreal quality wherein the known becomes unknown. Beams of sunlight swirling with dust silhouette darkly defined shapes, in stark contrast to the dimness of the woods. The time and weather of the day may also summon mystery, but these you cannot control. The most you can do is make yourself available to them. Dusk and dark night, rain and rolling mist imbue the landscape with an otherworldly air. In a familiar world, light is our friendly guide; in a mysterious garden, it is diffuse and uncertain at best.

Light in a garden characterized by mystery may play a variety of roles. As in the stairway of an abandoned house, the light may be spooky and thin, created by arching branches that obscure the sun in subtle ways. Or light and shadow may contrast resoundingly: brilliant rays of sunlight, breaking suddenly through a clearing, are nearly blinding. Washing over an ancient tree, the eye of the sun illuminates old scars and throws hidden nooks into deepest shadow. Shafts of sunlight mark the boundaries between familiar and unfamiliar. The outer margins of the well-lit world slip into dimness, and on from there into darkness.

To take full advantage of the power of light and shadow in your garden of mystery, plant groupings of trees that will create

LEFT: *Rich with age and use, an oil jar calls to mind the secrets of civilizations long past.* OPPOSITE: *On a hazy morning, Russian sage (Perovskia atriplicifolia) blurs alluringly. Without clear edges, mystery rises up majestically.*

The garden of mystery attracts us because it grants us a rare

opportunity to become adventurers;

it offers us a chance to appease our restless souls.

patterns of dappled light on the landscape below. Spacing the trees variably will result in unexpected showers of light juxtaposed by recesses of darkness. You might also consider some single trees or plantings of tall, distinctive perennials or grasses that will produce graceful outlines when limned by the rising or setting sun.

Arrayed on water, light creates magical illusions and adds reflections that melt onto the surface, mixing with leaves, swirls from the undertow, and plants around the water's edge. In striking opposition to the play of light on water is the mood of a dark pool. Black water circled by bright yellow leaves appears bottomless, hinting at a subterranean passageway. In such pools—as in old, clouded mirrors—you are never quite sure what image you might glimpse.

In the enigmatic landscape, a profound stillness descends gently. Though no garden is, nor should be, devoid of sound, the garden of mystery is wrapped in the hushed calm of a cathedral. Your yielding step on wet leaves, soft moss, quiet earth, seems the single link to the known world. As if understanding that we are here to explore, to find sanctuary, quiet sits patiently on her throne. She knows we need spaces between sounds to find comfort in an unfamiliar world. When a branch snaps with surprising finality, its echo leaves no trail. The mysterious garden gives you quiet so you *can* hear the crackle of a twig falling, the sudden swoosh of a startled bird.

Without a constant concert of sound, we can relax, giving ourselves space to explore. A quiet mind is a luxury in today's world. Eventually, we fit comfortably into long silences, finding solace and time to accept

OPPOSITE: *When planting a tree, imagine its limbs heavy with age, its canopy sprawling, and use this mental picture to place the tree properly.* LEFT: *Falling water sounds faintly like a faucet left to run carelessly—it hushes all other forest noises.* BELOW: *As dark and eerie as a witch's looking glass, the murky depths of this black pool beg to be disturbed with a fallen leaf or a daring toe.*

Shafts of sunlight mark the boundaries between familiar and unfamiliar.

The outer margins of the well-lit world slip into dimness,

and on from there into darkness.

new challenges. And then silence releases her grip; the quiet is broken by a sudden whistle of wind through a stand of pines, a branch snapping, grasses rippling and rustling. However startling these sounds may be in contrast to silence, they are infrequent.

To create the hush of the mysterious sanctuary, you might consider planting a woodland garden. Its dense, shady interior evokes expanses of undiscovered forests, carpeted with springy moss and generations of fallen leaves. If a woodland space is undesirable or impracticable, plant instead with an intent to muffle footsteps. Layers of foliage mute sound thoroughly; leave paths unpaved and encourage silence by removing bird and animal attractors to another part of the garden.

But stillness is not the only quality that pervades the mysterious sanctuary. A fragrance of damp earth—a scent like the underneath of stones, where insects rush—rises. The sirenesque perfume of a wisteria vine curls into your nostrils. Like an opiate, the scent ensnares you, drawing you from your stated purpose.

The sweet, headachy perfume of wisteria (Wisteria floribunda 'Royal Purple') will lure you from your path, sending you in pursuit of its celestial scent. Like lavender-pink boas draped across the crook of an arm, its flowers dangle elegantly from dark branches.

OPPOSITE: All plants, even those not usually thought of as fragrant, have their own special scents. The powdery petals of this bellflower (Campanula takesimana) droop in silent intensity, hiding their innermost parts and giving off a quiet perfume. RIGHT: Raindrops on Spanish flag (Ipomoea lobata), a member of the morning glory family, bring an aromatic freshness to the plump petals.

Plentiful foliage has its own smell, with a tangy or peppery quality that is as alluring as any flower but harder to identify.

Scent in this mysterious garden may be hidden or fleeting. It wafts across paths, emanates from beneath a tangle of shrubbery. This garden's perfume is arresting, but only briefly. It spins you for a moment, steering you from your course. Mixed with the wet, earthy smell of a forest floor, the aroma is more reminiscent of the earth's inner essence than of a typical garden where flower fragrances dominate. Nourishing our imaginations, the fragrances here, though subtle, are also enveloping. Caught unaware, we stand in frozen recollection, trying to place a fragrance, to connect it to what we

know. Delicate scents like these encourage us to search for their sources and reasons.

In the evening, the fragrance of flowers seems more mysterious because there is no visual guide; the senses of smell and touch are more acute. While all appears to be sleeping—plants curling into themselves, petals facing downward in repose—nothing, in fact, is. Dreamy and hypnotic, this realm lies beyond sleep. The delicate fragrance reminds you that nature's layers are infinite. If you were to drop to your knees and dig, new smells would be released, strong scents of working life beneath the earth's outermost skin.

To encourage subtle fragrance in your garden, limit yourself to just one or two types of flower per bloom period, and make sure that you choose ones that emit a signature perfume. Siting these plants in semi-hidden places, such as around the bend of a path or deep within a thicket of other plants, tantalizes visitors, luring them to discover the source of the scent. Plentiful foliage has its own smell, often with a tangy or peppery quality that is as alluring as any flower but harder to identify.

Mysteries lurk, too, in the undulating layers of color in a sanctuary garden. But

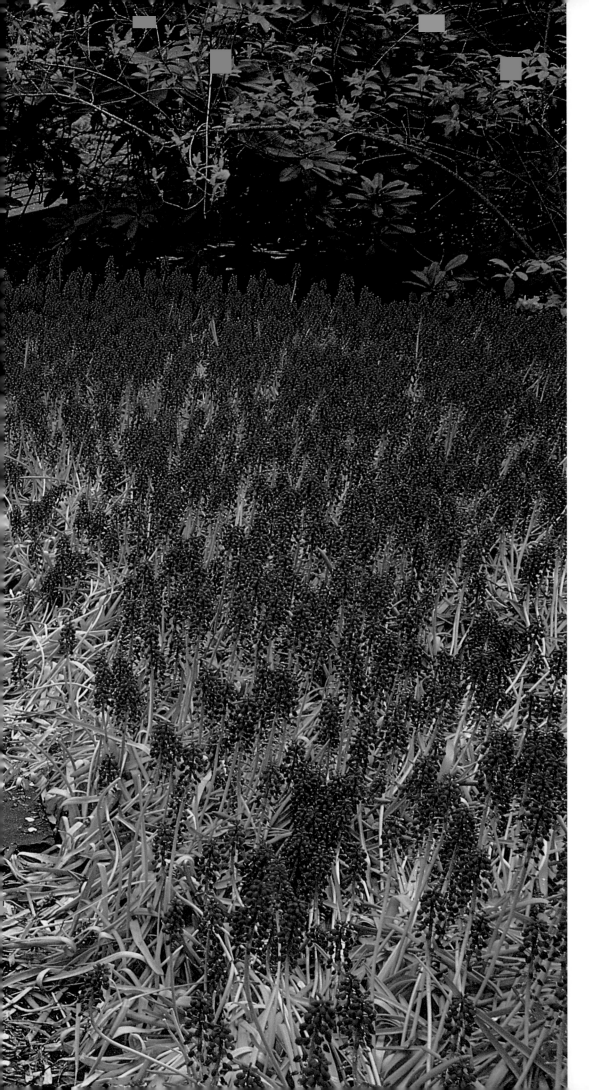

LEFT: *Grape hyacinth (Muscari 'Armeniacum') spreads like a royal velvet robe across the bare earth. Afraid to step and mar the rich texture, your feet keep to the well-worn path.* BELOW: *Chartreuse spikes of yellow-twig dogwood (Cornus stolonifera 'Flaviramea') grow in striking contrast to white snow. The firmly upright branches encourage alertness in the wintry landscape.*

these colors, like this sanctuary's sounds and scents, are subtle and hidden. Unlike other garden landscapes, the view does not shimmer with vibrant streaks of color. Instead, colors slide gently across surfaces. Pressed against the edge of a path, a wealth of hues, tints, and shades weave into a multi-toned blanket, enfolding you in a gentle gleam. Colors in this garden glow with the fire of fine jewels, rather than glittering sharply.

Colors also leap forth from unexpected sources. Leaf surfaces are painted with darkened shadows and valleys. Thousands of green tints—pale, bright, dark, or with shades of blue and yellow—are reflected.

They ripple with variation. Their veins contrast strikingly with the foliage, adding colored webs when illuminated.

Other hues—blue, purple, pink, and cream—lie in wait behind branches and fronds. When lifted and parted, the boughs reveal the ornate anatomy of the flowers tucked within, hiding yet another universe of color. Concealed beneath bent limbs, caramel-and-cream-colored cones dance in unison when limbs are jostled, and drop to the ground with a heavy thump.

Pattern adorns the living walls in this intimate garden. Tendrils of green tease you through the landscape. Completely

enveloped, you are startled by the complicated order of this living web. Above and around you, leaves fit and slip into one another like the surface of a puzzle, edges lifted and outlined slightly. A lattice of limbs overhead crosses wildly, zigzagging in tones of sepia and black. Foliage textures and shapes—serrated ovals, smooth hearts, rough blades—create living sculpture.

Unable to see where plants begin and end, you stand in stillness, trying to sort the tangle. Soft and organic, shapes are masked by overgrowth. What lies beneath these green mounds is a mystery. As if at a masquerade ball, you stand in suspense, guess-

Often surreal, a mysterious landscape delights us even though we cannot always comprehend the pattern of nature's weave.

ing at possible identities beneath the lushly costumed plants.

Creating layered tunnels, vines spin and knit themselves around trees, plugging lighted holes. Espaliered trees, twisted by age and circumstance, mask fences and gates. Pendulous branches sweep over paths, obscuring well-traveled routes. Bending and rising under their own weight, they open and close like gates. Often surreal, a mysterious landscape delights us even though we cannot always comprehend the pattern of nature's weave. We may never grasp all of a garden's mysterious ways, though we do not deny ourselves the pleasure of trying.

At one time or another, we have all peeked through the bars of a wrought-iron gate, down a narrow alley, or through a window set in battered wood, desperate to know what lies within. Gates and doors are symbols of beginnings, clear markers of a new journey undertaken. Such thresholds beckon us forward tauntingly; we are beset with curiosity. Whether discreetly or boldly, entrances and exits announce themselves as boundaries to new territory. In the garden, we recognize a separate world entered by crossing these thresholds.

In addition to marking the entrance to your garden with a gateway, you might design

ABOVE: *A tingle of anticipation runs the length of your back as you reach for the latch; nothing piques curiosity quite like a latched gate or a closed door.* RIGHT: *The quiet mystery of ancient ferns and dripping Spanish moss are complemented by a towering, curving branch and a circle of trees over blackened water. Given the courage to explore, one treads joyously toward the unfamiliar world.*

LEFT: *Woodland gardens lend themselves to gentle walkways, and indeed every woodland garden must have a path. This one, made of moss and wide, flat steps, is a wonderful entry point into a sheltering forest.*
OPPOSITE: *Private sanctuaries, hidden from prying eyes and removed from the clamor of people, allow us to focus intently on the living world.*

a path that flows through it. Twists and turns along the path inspire a sense of wonder, an interest in the outcome. A fallen tree, a grouping of rocks, or a jutting pot may impede the path. In order to move beyond this puzzling new piece, we are forced to make still more choices. Large obstacles slow our progress: we are not always prepared for these, preferring to move swiftly and serenely along our route. But such obstacles represent opportunities to stop and appreciate our surroundings. They also suggest alternatives—

we may set a different course altogether or we may simply pause before surmounting the impediment and continuing on our way.

Safe in the care of your oft-used intuition, you may wish to venture off the path. At first, your feet may lead you cautiously, veering only inches from the well-worn walk to inspect a seedpod or wildflower. Eventually, though, hesitancy will give way to curiosity and finally to outright boldness. You will search eagerly for new or disguised artifacts and objects along the route,

pulling away vines, peering into caverns, pushing limbs out of the way. Hidden, their beauty is intensified; we cherish these objects more because they have been painstakingly uncovered.

Along the path, an arbor, gazebo, or bench hides occupants from prying eyes. An arbor or gazebo will take you, too, into its confidence, with whispers of past conversations and suggestions of long-ago visitors. In sheltered niches, you steal moments, pausing to satiate your senses, soak in fresh new details. Natural structures, divides, and small openings along your route also provoke investigation. You push your body through layers of trees, foliage, and bushes before disappearing into a green abyss.

Life is not meant to be carefully planned and ever familiar—
we must trust that we will survive strange journeys.

Some secret spots are just big enough to accommodate your scrunched form. Others run up against a quiet pond or trickling stream, allowing for rest. Like silence, such niches give peace after focused concentration, a moment to recall and refuel. Tucked into the landscape, they allow for unencumbered introspection, a chance to rediscover yourself—unafraid, curious, and provoked by mystery.

To give into irresistible curiosity, to visit a mysterious garden for a little while, is to live more deeply. Finding our way in this alien world, letting go of the familiar things we desperately cling to, brings richness and courage into our lives. Life is not meant to be carefully planned and ever familiar—we must trust that we will survive strange journeys. Landscapes full of mystery allow us to focus our energies on the living world

around us. Here, we shift our attention toward learning and experiencing, becoming intimately connected with the journey. The twists and turns of a garden's mysterious routes are not unlike life's path. Unaware of what life holds for us, we travel onward. Resting occasionally in seclusion, we regroup. Centered, we navigate challenges and adventures, just as we traverse the wilds of the mysterious sanctuary.

CHAPTER FIVE

CONTEMPLA

Reclining amidst tall-stemmed verbena, your clangorous thoughts begin to yield to calmness. An insect stilled on a slender grass blade breathes in subdued potential; its presence, too, quiets you. Where has your mind wandered? How have its rhythms slowed? Think, for a moment, about the power of focus. When you lock your eyes on an object or a scene, the rest of the world fades into the background. Gradually, that point becomes your world. The literal image dissolves, and you are free to simply be, liberated from the tangle of everyday cares. To achieve this state of mind is to find balance, harmony, and peace.

We may seek a quiet spot so that we can reflect upon a specific problem or consider the direction of our lives. By eliminating one by one the daily distractions we all face, we can better focus on solutions to our troubles. Soul-searching is a healthy pursuit; it is natural and right to look for ways to add meaning to our lives.

A period of contemplation is enriching no matter our particular goals, but finding places upon our earth to help ease ourselves into a contemplative mood may present a challenge. Our gardens, our precious personal landscapes, are ideal spots for reflection because of the abundance of beautiful objects upon which we may focus.

Yet not all gardens, however beautiful, encourage contemplation. The passionate garden, for example, is too noisy, too bright, and too rich with heady perfumes. Once there, we are prompted to act with excitement. A mysterious garden, though it may encourage introspection, proposes an exploration of the landscape rather than the self. Even peaceful gardens, quiet and restful as they are, don't necessarily contain contemplative elements. While we may come away from a contemplative garden feeling more peaceful than usual, it is because we have explored our selves and arrived at new perspectives that bring balance to our lives. We feel at peace because we have worked to achieve this state, rather than been inspired to it by our surroundings alone.

Designing a garden space that encourages meditation and reflection is a fine art, and the garden artist has many ingredients that can help effect what noted garden designer and author Julie Moir Messervy has termed a "mind journey." She explains that when you come to a place where a scene or object seizes your attention and becomes the focus for contemplation, you travel on "a voyage of the spirit through space, [that] engages your mind rather than your feet or senses." In a sense, you read the garden, your eyes stopping at particular points along the way, lingering on specific objects that inspire your mind's voyage.

To create a space for contemplation, balance elements designed to evoke

ABOVE: *High points that reach far above other flowers, like this camas (Camassia leichtlinii 'Caerulea'), catch our wandering gaze.*
OPPOSITE: *In this Japanese-inspired design, a central accent placed on a small island of flowers and foliage encourages focus.*

Soul-searching is a healthy pursuit;

it is natural and right to look for ways to add meaning to our lives.

quietude with those that spell energy. Remember that inanimate objects have their own "energy"; through their color, flowing lines, or tactile natures, they affect the people who view them.

To feed the contemplative mind, choose focal objects for your garden—sculptures, large rocks, simple fountains, and found objects are just a few possibilities. Place them in sympathy with each other and with the landscape, remembering that a sense of movement is important. When the garden is viewed from afar, the objects should seem to draw the eye through the space. A closer view should allow you to focus on one piece alone, absorbing its particular energy and beauty. Arrange the space to please yourself, and you will surely enchant visitors as well.

Plants, too, may be used as focal points in the garden—consider a tree, a stand of grasses, or a dramatic planting of a single type of flower. Or, as you muse in your contemplative garden, you may choose to focus on just one plant (whether or not it is, in fact, an acknowledged focal point) or even a single part of a plant. The intricacy of a blooming flower stuns you with the miracle of the world's complexity. Its petals, with their papery aspect and labyrinthine veins, draw a steady gaze.

BELOW: *A smooth blue stone arranged provocatively beside a grass blade has a dynamic presence all its own.* OPPOSITE, TOP: *Like a misplaced megalith from Stonehenge, this rock stands steadfast and true in a changing landscape.* OPPOSITE, BOTTOM: *Rippling stone surfaces come alive in the light of the sun, evoking strength and potential energy.*

Remember that inanimate objects have

their own "energy"; through their color,

flowing lines, or tactile natures,

they affect the people who view them.

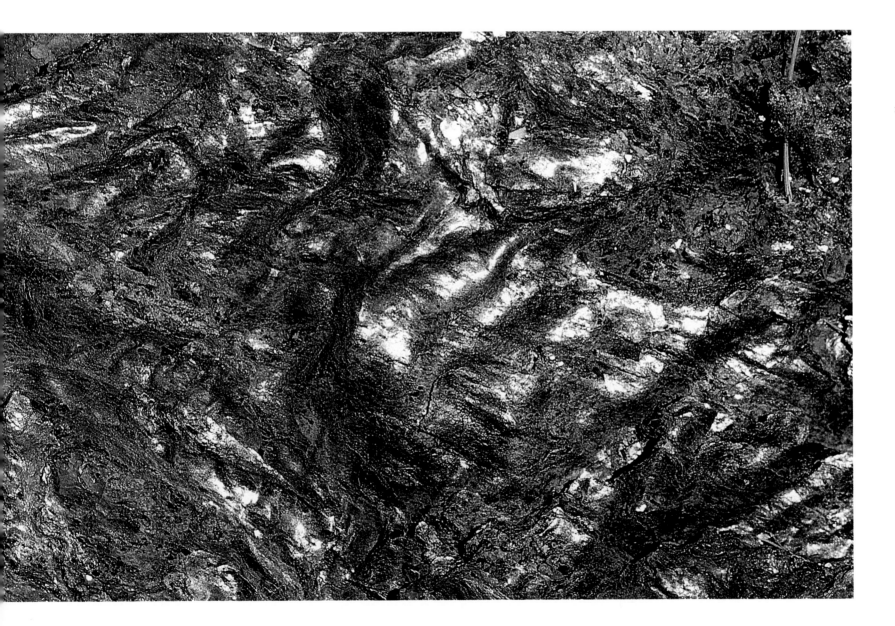

If you've not already wondered at the miraculous ways nature perpetuates life, look no further than your garden for a thorough investigation. LEFT: Angel's trumpet (Brugmansia candida) bows its lovely head. BELOW: Red petals and crimson-veined sepals of bee balm (Monarda didyma 'Gardenview') reach beseechingly toward the viewer. OPPOSITE: The graphic form and burnt orange tones of a daylily (Hemerocallis 'Krakatoa Lava') are a wonder to behold.

Water somehow combines dramatic energy with perfect tranquillity. Like fire, its transparency and fluidity are endlessly fascinating.

Water ranks high in the pantheon of garden elements, and it is wonderfully appropriate in the contemplative garden. For centuries, garden designers have relied upon its spirit of restfulness. Water somehow combines dramatic energy with perfect tranquillity. Like fire, its transparency and fluidity are endlessly fascinating. Installing a small pool, upon which will be reflected the movement of the clouds or the waving of the grasses, is like setting a small mirror into the ground—this singular element brings together heaven and earth. Or you may prefer a crystal stream of falling water, with its implications of eternity.

Contrast and harmony are themes that will aid you in arranging both your focal points and your plants—think of smooth stones beside silkily flowing water, brilliant-petaled flowers against a backdrop of dark evergreen leaves, or an intensely vertical statue within a bed of creeping roses. Create pairings that soothe, and juxtapose them with other pairings designed to provoke.

Include in your sanctuary garden, if possible, a seat from which you may launch your contemplative journey. A seat or bench sets up a vantage point that outlines the boundaries of the garden, limiting vistas and defining the space as distinct from other

FAR LEFT: *Tightly stacked stones, partnered with high-growing* Rodgersia *and other bog-loving plants, set off a calm and reflective pond.* LEFT: *Clear water pouring in a silver stream refreshes and restores in utter simplicity.*

122

C
O
N
T
E
M
P
L
A
T
I
O
N

places. Made from aged wood, stone, wicker, or iron—and perhaps sheltered from sun, rain, or watchful eyes by a canopy of flow-ers—benches offer charming secret medita-tion spots.

Seated, your limbs relax, your eyes take in the scene around you, and you begin to ease comfortably into reflection. Your body, now cradled by a seat, is more apt to release its tension, to become still for your mind's travels. Seats and benches should be posi-tioned to view important features or areas of the garden, or set in front of specific focal

points. By narrowing somewhat your point of view, a seat can open your mind's own landscape, where unexplored valleys arise and your contemplative journey begins.

Whether a garden embraces symmetry or asymmetry also determines how easily the mind slips into contemplation. Features that mirror each other are pleasing to the eye and represent the human ideal of beau-ty. But this does not mean that you must plan your garden with a formal symmetry in mind. Even the smallest details—the uni-form arrangement of petals on a flower

head or the stepped branches of a towering pine—can celebrate nature's fondness for regular patterns.

Allow the governing forces of balance in the garden to lead your thoughts, and realize that every aspect of the garden can serve as a metaphor for our own lives. Waterdrops bal-anced along a leaf's edge show astounding precision and balance. The perched pearls of water, in their precarious position, are nothing short of miraculous; curving, sensu-ous lines of droplets and leaf contours are nearly dazzling. How did nature construct

A seat or bench sets up a vantage point that
outlines the boundaries of the garden, limiting vistas
and defining the space as distinct from other places.

The elegance of balanced water droplets, poised per-fectly upon a leaf's edge, echoes the miracles of equi-librium that nature achieves in ways large and small throughout the universe.

126

CONTEMPLATION

such perfection? The delicate symmetry of this miniature still life seems so simple, so pure—but we know instinctively that such a tableau cannot last. Such a scene can stir ruminations on balance and beauty in our own lives, leading us to an appreciation of special moments as they are presented to us.

While the uniformity and proportion of traditional symmetry are effortless to view, helping to ease us into a reflective state, asymmetry in the contemplative garden is also riveting. Unrelated elements without obvious sameness in size, shape, or position can come together beautifully as a balanced whole. Lines and circles complement each other; oddly shaped pieces beside a symmetrical sculpted form work surprisingly well together; an upright, formal chair placed in

a field of wildflowers seems a perfect fit. The key is to create an uncontrived look where the objects exist in natural harmony—just because the pieces are not identical does not mean they should not be balanced. One way to achieve this harmony is by selecting pieces that have one element in common; perhaps they share an earthy terra-cotta hue or a strongly horizontal plane, though they are of vastly different sizes and shapes. Such points capture the eye, guiding it successfully through an assortment of objects and an asymmetrical garden design.

One garden aesthetic that has perfected the subtle art of creating balance, symmetry, and asymmetry is that associated with the Japanese school of design. Many Japanese gardens embody techniques and plantings

designed specifically to elicit a contemplative state of mind.

A distinctive feature of Japanese gardens is the manner in which natural materials are used to symbolize and suggest the beauty of nature. In one type of Japanese garden, various materials such as rocks, trees, earth, and moss are used to form an ideal landscape in miniature. In other designs, rocks are emphasized, creating rhythm by virtue of their various sizes and shapes. Providing a distinct frame for the garden, rocks give impressionistic and realistic representations in the garden. Because Japanese garden designers treat stones as materials that have vital qualities, the stones may be used to illustrate life, soul, and water, with careful consideration given to their placement.

Water is intrinsic to Japanese design because it enlivens and revives the garden, but it need not be present literally. Water may be represented by patterns raked carefully into sand or gravel to imitate water flow, tides, and ripples. In a Japanese meditation garden, a tree trunk, placed in a raked field of gravel, stands with silent intensity.

Again, this garden is designed to be used as a refuge from the demands of everyday life. Other elements that provoke thoughtful focus in Japanese gardens are bridges, lanterns, stone basins, and bamboo, cleverly designed for a multitude of garden features. In each of these materials resides the potential energy to animate the reflective mind.

In Japanese gardens, we observe an attitude in which nature is joined with everyday living. To the Japanese, a garden is not only a place to cultivate trees and flowering plants, it is also a space for rest, repose, and mediation. Like some other contemplative settings, the grounds of a Japanese temple are a sacred space in which nature is considered the deity.

In Japanese gardens, we observe an attitude in
which nature is joined with everyday living.

*In Japanese garden design,
rocks are an integral material
and are used in nearly every
garden. The rocks' placement is
part of an intricate symbolism
reflecting Eastern philosophies
about life and nature's cycles.*

Here, each individual prepares him- or herself to enter into a different state of being and worship by symbolically cleansing the mind, spirit, and body. In a temple, as in many other Japanese gardens, a water basin for cleansing is an integral part of the sanctuary. Often, a narrow footpath leads to a traditional stone basin, complete with a bamboo cane—out of which runs clear water—and a dipper, inviting you to rinse your hands and mouth.

Truly appreciating a Japanese garden's offerings depends on an understanding of the space. While the pure openness of Japanese gardens easily draws most into a contemplative state, a deeper knowledge of Japanese design principles will lead to a more transcendent experience. The philosophy implies that only those who mentally complete the incomplete can discover true beauty. A quote from a periodical of the Ryoanji

Temple, site of perhaps the most famous Zen garden, illustrates beautifully a contemplative experience in a Japanese garden:

When we face this garden and are struck by the calm, pure and noble sincerity of the absolute self, we, the individual egos, have our stained minds purified and get the quality of the Buddha, basking in the blessing of our pure minds and this is the zenith of Zen teachings.

ABOVE LEFT: *A rustic bench and arbor covered with morning glories offer a secluded spot for contemplation.* ABOVE RIGHT: *Trees and sky mirrored in a small pool bring the heavens down to earth.* RIGHT: *A tiny stone wrapped with twine makes a delicate accent for a bed of moss.* OPPOSITE: *Dippers and running water encourage symbolic cleansing, after which one is free to cross the threshold into a new state of consciousness.*

While Eastern cultures have a long and well-developed tradition of meditative spaces, many other cultures have evolved their own ways of turning inward toward an exploration of the self. For thousands of years, labyrinths have existed as mysterious symbols of uncertain origin, and have recently been rediscovered by those seeking meaningful quiet space. We can still see ancient labyrinth designs—which probably evolved from simple spirals—carved onto rocks, sketched on walls as graffiti, and patterned on coins and seals.

Most of the labyrinths we see today are based on one of two designs: the Cretan, a classical seven-ring labyrinth design found on ancient Cretan coins; or the Chartres, from a medieval eleven-circuit labyrinth design in the floor of Chartres Cathedral in France. Depending on the culture or geographic location, labyrinths were used for spiritual journeys, religious ceremonies, and other rituals. Whatever their particular use, the power of labyrinths has endured throughout human history.

Labyrinths designed for garden sanctuaries are often created using natural materials, such as grasses, flowers, rocks, or other garden riches. Though a labyrinth may not be immediately recognized as a traditional garden element, if we define "garden" as a natural refuge from the surrounding world, where cycles of change are clear and beauty is found in every twist and turn, then indeed labyrinths are inspired choices for garden spaces.

A labyrinth is a set of complex geometric paths with its design based on the archetypal patterns of nature. While they are often confused with mazes, labyrinths are quite different. Mazes, with their multitude of routes and tricky dead ends, are puzzles intended to confuse and mystify their occupants. Labyrinths, on the other hand, are designed with contemplation in mind. Each has only one path, which leads into the center and back out.

RIGHT: *Modeled after the famous labyrinth at the Chartres Cathedral in France, the design of this eleven-circuit labyrinth goes back thousands of years.* OPPOSITE: *This turf pattern is a maze rather than a labyrinth, which is characterized by only one way to enter and exit. The maze shown here offers immediate choices.*

A labyrinth features no cunning deceptions—in fact there are no geographic decisions to make at all. The circle, the defining shape of a labyrinth, is a well-known meditational symbol and an excellent shape to integrate into a contemplative garden. Circles have been called the most meditative pattern on earth, as they are whole and without breaks, signifying eternity and the completeness of the universe. Because of its circular pattern, a labyrinth is a useful place for walking meditations; an even-paced journey leads to a single goal, the labyrinth's center. Those who walk labyrinths say that the exercise focuses the mind, slows the breathing, and induces a peaceful, meditative state.

A growing number of people are rediscovering the labyrinth as a path to prayer, introspection, and emotional healing. The Reverend Dr. Lauren Artress, a leader in the revival of the labyrinth explains, "When you walk into a labyrinth, the mind quiets and you begin to see what's happening inside. You become transparent to yourself.

Circles have been called the most meditative pattern on earth, as they are whole and without breaks, signifying eternity and the completeness of the universe.

ABOVE: *This eleven-circuit labyrinth is influenced by Japanese design principles; its surface is made with decomposed granite and two thousand bricks that edge the path.*

RIGHT: *This rounding, mounding labyrinth encourages a thoughtful walk in an open environment. Its soft texture and wonderful country location surely help visitors find patience and peace.*

You can see that you are scared or frightened or that you lack courage....You can see your judgments against people and against yourself."

A walk through a labyrinth works to produce a reflective state of mind in the same way that a focal object invites introspection. In a labyrinth, as in a garden setting, you can seek sanctuary from your daily routine. Your mind empties itself of distracting thoughts, so that you emerge tranquil, open to new ideas, and willing to explore your inner self.

Perhaps the most fascinating thing about these curving pathways is that they are intended for movement—they are as compelling as the onward and relentless pace of time. Because you must move to appreciate a labyrinth, it is a wonderful alternative for those of us who become restless when forced to sit still, even when we are surrounded by the most stunning of garden scenes.

A typical labyrinth contains twists and turns, hairpin bends, and definite angles shaped from concentric circles or "circuits."

Depending upon the number of circuits and your personal pace, a walk through a labyrinth can take anywhere from a few minutes to an hour or more. You can walk through or run through, depending on your level of energy and enthusiasm or your spiritual needs.

The onward movement through the labyrinth allows us the luxury of space and time to reflect on our lives, our choices, and our relationships. Walking a labyrinth need not be a solitary experience. Traveling the path with another person can expand awareness in new ways, as we react to and absorb the energies of the people around us.

You can create your own labyrinth, however large or small, in your garden, backyard, living room floor, or on a canvas to pack up and carry with you. Making your own labyrinth can be rewarding and need not be complicated. By mounding earth in one of the labyrinth patterns, you can create a "country" labyrinth. Plant grass or wildflower seeds along the mounds to make a meadow garden that blends in with the surrounding area. If you like, you can create a firmer, sturdier labyrinth by lining the walls of the earthen mounds with stones. When you have more time, you can also line the paths with small stones, granite chips, or flagstone. This helps stabilize the mounds, prevents water evaporation, and insulates the mound's interior. Maintaining this country labyrinth is also easy: simply trim the grasses and flowers if they grow too high. For even simpler labyrinths, use chalk or paint to outline the shape, or collect rocks or seashells from the beach to use as markers.

Unlike some transitions—in which the ending is an unsettling question mark—the labyrinth provides a single, known goal, the center of the circle.

OPPOSITE: *With patience and planning, you can make your own labyrinth. This one is made more beautiful by autumn leaves, which have colored pathways with orange, yellow, and brown.*
LEFT: *Stones, bricks, and grass are carefully laid out in a seven-circuit labyrinth. Along these circular pathways a growing number of people have rediscovered the ancient pattern as a path to prayer, introspection, and emotional healing.*

137

C
O
N
T
E
M
P
L
A
T
I
O
N

CONCLUSION

Dream. Reflect. Breathe. Contemplate. Taking moments to restore yourself and to study your potential should be as commonplace as sleeping—the time we spend in a sanctuary garden is precious. Like a journal writer who recalls memories and learns about him- or herself by reading past entries, those of us who visit spiritual landscapes learn to locate the place in our minds where we can evaluate the progress of our lives—these self-observations are crucial to growth and to making positive future choices. A sanctuary garden frames our thoughts, offers us a symbolic threshold, and provides blank pages across which we can scrawl our most private dreams.

Enveloped in the sights, scents, and sounds of the sanctuary garden, we can relax and absorb the complexities of worlds both inner and outer.

Living in New York City overwhelms me at times. The cacophony of sights, sounds, and smells sometimes triggers sensory over-load. My life in the city is a sharp contrast to my life growing up on a large farm in Connecticut where, instead of dodging messengers riding bicycles on the sidewalk, I walked with head down looking for arrow-heads with my grandmother. My parents owned a nursery and greenhouses. As a child I often stood on a stool beside my father repotting geraniums. The smell of the tightly packed earth and the warm humidity of the greenhouse lingers in my memory. In fact, many memories of peace and solitude stand out in those first ten years of my life—riding my bicycle to a spe-cial blackberry bush gleaming in the sum-mer sun and picking a warm berry to eat on the spot, wandering through orchards fragrant with the fullness of ripening apples, and the dusty feel of the kicked-up clods of dirt clinging to my white socks. The intense focus upon the small things in nature shaped a large part of my child-hood. Nature was also my escape and refuge. Especially when my father was diagnosed with cancer, and our house became quiet with waiting. After he died we sold the farm and moved to the suburbs of a major city. Though I have lived in and traveled to many places, my heart continues to seek and find sanctuary in nature.

Today my work as a garden photogra-pher has brought me full circle, offering me opportunities to reconnect with nature. Looking into the depths and pat-terns of flowers and plants through my camera lens reveals a world both known and unknown. As I focus solely upon the beauty before me there is a moment of connection, and time stands still. I also relish those special moments in a garden that does not loudly proclaim its design, but rather welcomes me by its naturalness and simplicity. Discovering grasses swaying in the breeze, listening to the gentle sounds of water, becoming aware of a sud-den scent of lilac or lavender, looking into a dark pool with mysterious depths—all evoke moments of serenity.

Not surprisingly, researching gardens to photograph for this book led me to many beautiful and peaceful places. As I pho-tographed, head down, intensely focused on the splendor before me, I felt nourished and at home. However, I became aware that this wasn't enough. I was experiencing a mid-life spiritual emptiness. I realized that I had been too narrowly focused for too long.

At about this time a friend mentioned her experience walking an outdoor meditation labyrinth. She explained how walking the labyrinth helped her answer difficult questions. A labyrinth sounded like a good place to nurture my own personal growth.

In my research I learned that Wisdom House Retreat and Conference Center in Litchfield, Connecticut, had installed a seven-circuit labyrinth. My excitement mounted after I received permission to walk and photograph it. What I saw upon arriving at the Wisdom House labyrinth was a circular grass path marked by brick and stone set into the ground. With open views of the Litchfield Hills, this was not a maze with claustrophobic high hedges and confusing dead ends.

Taking the first step on the path was difficult, just like all my first steps or attempts at something new. I made my way into the center and cried unexpectedly. I retraced my steps and walked out. What was the powerful energy that I could almost see radiating upwards and outward from my head? It was as if my focus had suddenly shifted from close-up to panoramic. My sense of space changed.

That first labyrinth walk has led me to many other labyrinths throughout the country. Walking them has been a gift to my spirit. When I first had the idea of a book about sanctuary gardens I wasn't sure where I would photograph. I only knew that certain gardens and flowers had always provided me with nourishment and that I wanted to share my vision with others. *Sanctuary* is that vision and my gift to you.

—Dency Kane

Bennett, Jennifer. *Our Gardens, Ourselves*. Ontario, Calif.: Camden House, Camden East, 1994.

Brookes, John. *The Country Garden*. New York: Crown Publishers, 1987.

Cox, Jeffrey. *Creating a Garden for the Senses*. New York: Abbeville Press, 1993.

Crandall, Chuck and Barbara. *Creating Privacy in the Garden*. New York: Rizzoli, 1997.

Dillon, Helen. *Garden Artistry*. New York: MacMillan, 1995.

Don, Montagu. *Sensuous Garden*. New York: Simon and Schuster, 1997.

Druse, Ken. *Natural Shade Garden*. New York: Clarkson Potter Publishers, 1992.

Eck, Joe, drawings by Lisa Brooks. *Elements of Garden Design*. New York: Henry Holt & Company, 1996.

Eliade, Mircea. *The Sacred and the Profane*. New York: Harcourt, Brace, 1959.

Fisher, Adrian, with photographs by Georg Gerster. *Labyrinth: Solving the Riddle of the Maze*. New York: Harmony Books, 1990.

Gerlac-Spriggs, Nancy, Richard Enoch Kaufman, and Sam Bass Warner. *Restorative Gardens: The Healing Landscape*. New Haven, Conn.: Yale University Press, 1998.

Graham, Rose, with illustrations by Paul Cox. *The Romantic Garden: A Guide to Creating a Beautiful and Private Garden Paradise*. New York: Viking, 1988.

Hill, Thomas, edited and with an introduction by Richard Mabey. *The Gardener's Labyrinth*. New York: Oxford University Press, 1987.

Hobhouse, Penelope. *Penelope Hobhouse's Gardening Through the Ages*. New York: Simon and Schuster, 1992.

Kan Yashiroda, guest editor, Peter K. Nelson, associate editor, Takuma P. Tono and the editorial committee of the Brooklyn Botanical Garden. *Japanese Gardens and Miniature Landscapes*, a special printing of *Plants and Gardens*, Vol. 17, No. 3. Brooklyn, New York: The Brooklyn Botanical Garden.

Lawson, Andrew. *The Gardener's Book of Color*. Pleasantville, New York: Reader's Digest Association, Inc., 1996.

Malitz, Jerome. *Personal Landscapes*. Portland, Oregon: Timber Press, 1989.

McDowell, Christopher Forest, and Tricia Clark McDowell. *The Sanctuary Garden*. New York: Fireside, 1998.

Messervy, Julie Moir, with illustrations by Barbara M. Berger. *The Magic Land: Designing Your Own Enchanted Garden*. New York: MacMillan, 1998.

Messervy, Julie Moir, with photographs by Sam Abell. *The Inward Garden*. Boston: Little, Brown and Company, 1995.

Mitchell, William J., Charles W. Moore, William Turnbull, Jr. *The Poetics of Gardens*. Cambridge, Mass.: The MIT Press, 1988.

Olwell, Carol. *Gardening From the Heart: Why Gardeners Garden*. Berkeley, Calif.: Antelope Island Press, 1990.

Owen, Jane. *Eccentric Garden*. New York: Villard Books, 1990.

Pollan, Michael. *Second Nature*. New York: Dell Publishing, 1991.

Ravenna and Samnartini. *Secret Gardens of Venice*. Venice: Asenale & Editrice, 1996.

Ross, Stephanie. *What Gardens Mean*. Chicago: The University of Chicago Press, 1998.

Schinz, Marina, and Susan Littlefield. *Visions of Paradise: Themes and Variations on the Garden*. New York: Stewart, Tabori, and Chang, 1985.

Spier, Carol. *For Your Garden: Seats and Benches*. Boston: Little Brown and Company, 1994.

Ziegler, Catherine. *The Harmonious Garden: Color, Form, and Texture*. Portland, Oregon: Timber Press, 1996.

INDEX